John Geddie

The Lake Regions of Central Africa

A Record of Modern Discovery

John Geddie

The Lake Regions of Central Africa
A Record of Modern Discovery

ISBN/EAN: 9783744752688

Printed in Europe, USA, Canada, Australia, Japan

Cover: Foto ©Andreas Hilbeck / pixelio.de

More available books at **www.hansebooks.com**

THE LAKE REGIONS

OF

CENTRAL AFRICA.

A Record of Modern Discovery.

By *JOHN GEDDIE.*

WITH THIRTY-TWO ILLUSTRATIONS.

London:
T. NELSON AND SONS, PATERNOSTER ROW.
EDINBURGH; AND NEW YORK.

1883

Contents.

PART THIRD.

THE ZAMBESI.

List of Illustrations.

LAKE REGIONS OF CENTRAL AFRICA.

Introductory and Historical.

" Pistol. A fontra for the world and worldlings base !
I speak of Africa and golden joys."
2 Henry IV.

FRICA is the continent with which man—civilized man—has had perhaps the longest acquaintance, and concerning which he still knows least. It has been a mystery to him since the earliest ages, and he is only now beginning to penetrate the real heart of the secret. Probably it was on the rich soil of Egypt that the first geographer traced the first chart, and the first astronomer began to take observations of the sun, moon, and stars ; and it may have been on the flood of the Nile that the first mariner dared to trust himself on the fickle bosom of the waters. Since then the searchers after knowledge have gone far afield, and learned much. New worlds have been discovered and peopled, and the whole face of nature has been changed. But it was only the

other day that the hoary secret of the Nile—the distant and hidden sources from which Egypt draws its life-blood—was revealed; and it is around these very sources that the geographer and the naturalist have still the largest field for discovery, where the fairest promise is held out to the traveller and the hunter for "big game," and where a little romance continues to linger in a work-a-day world. It is strange that this should be so,—that the Nile, the water of which was used to knead the bricks of ancient Egypt, and that witnessed the rise of the pyramids, whose shapes can be seen glimmering in the gray dawn of history, should have been so long shrouded in mystery, while the course of the Mississippi, the existence of which was only ascertained some three and a half centuries ago, should be as familiarly known as that of the Rhine. On the whole, perhaps, it is fortunate that the secret has been so well kept. It will only be after everything has been "found out" that people will begin to understand the value of the unknown, and to sigh because there are no new lakes, rivers, and mountain ranges to discover. Meanwhile there is still a great deal that we should like to know, and cannot. Within the four corners of Africa, and more especially in the great equatorial Lake Region, there is a vast storehouse of unrevealed facts—an almost exhaustless possibility of discovery and adventure. So recently have the physical conditions of its interior been revealed, that Europe is still but half awake to the fact that Africa is green and flourishing at the heart, however uninviting in the rind; that

away in its centre, beyond the pestilential mangrove
swamps and tracts of arid sand that almost everywhere girdle its coasts, there are high and delightful
countries, full of running streams and far-stretching
lakes, of rich tropical verdure and abundant animal
life. It is too soon yet to pronounce an opinion on
the capabilities of Central Africa for supporting a
peaceful, industrious, and civilized population. The
climate of its uplands is no doubt more cool and
healthy than that of the coast, but its suitability for
European constitutions is at least doubtful. Still, it
is impossible not to believe that its magnificent lake
system, its mighty rivers, and its vast and fertile
plains will be employed for the uses of commerce and
agriculture, and that its future will be as brilliant as
its past has been dark.

The truth is that our ideas of Africa are still coloured with the old impressions of it which we find
in books and in the popular memory. The sunburned
and dusty face which it presented towards the Mediterranean photographed itself, as it were, on the
imagination of Europe. Our ancestors knew only
one side of it—the burned side—and they judged of
the whole from what they saw. To them Africa was
the "Desert," with a narrow fringe of vegetation
along its seaboard and in the Valley of the Nile,
and its " burning sand " was the image that presented
itself most naturally to the average mind. Now a
desert is all very well in its way—in the way, that is,
of thrilling adventure and hairbreadth escape; and
Africa is especially well provided in the matter of

deserts.   The Sahara is the greatest, the most unmitigated desert in the world.   It stretches from Tunis to Lake Chad, and from the Atlantic to the Nile— nay, it may be said to extend to the banks of the Tigris, for the Red Sea is only a depression in its surface that happens to be below the sea-level. There are other portions of its area which are supposed to be below the level of the Atlantic and the Mediterranean, and which science may one day transform into a new " Lake Region."   Geologists indeed inform us that the Sahara is the bed of an ancient sea, and its whole appearance and condition bear out the theory.   There is no regular rainfall or perennial streams; there are mountains, but no mountain systems, and there are, as has been said, depressions, but no permanent lakes.   Lastly, in the Sahara proper there are no stationary habitations, and few traces of animal or vegetable life.   In all these respects it not only differs from, but is a complete contrast to, the high, luxuriant, well-watered table-land below the Equator.

The picturesque sights of the desert have been made familiar enough to us by description: the long line of laden camels threading their way across the level waste, between the white blaze of the sun and the yellow glare of the sand, past the bleached skeletons of man and beast that strew the track; the vivid contrast of the flowing white robes and tawny faces of the Arab drivers and the ebony limbs of the negro slaves and attendants; the flight of a party of Moorish horsemen with their gay caparisons and glittering

CARAVAN CROSSING THE NUBIAN DESERT.

Page 15.

spears; the sand pillars, "leagued to fight with war-
ring winds;" the oases with their green palm-groves
and cool fountains; and the brilliant hues of a stormy
sunset. These, however, are but the accidents of
desert-life. Its characteristic aspect is silence, monotony, desolation. Even the beasts of prey avoid it.
Only for man, who finds an intellectual pleasure
in overcoming difficulty and facing Nature in her
sternest mood, can it have attractions; and the edge
of his appetite for travel is soon blunted by actual
experience of desert dangers and fatigues, when there
is no hope ahead to allure his steps forward.

Such was the main cause that discouraged African
exploration down to about the middle of the fifteenth
century. A new motive then came strongly into
play,—the rivalry of the European nations for the
trade of the East. There is a circumstantial ancient
story of a Phœnician vessel, sent out by Pharaoh
Necho, that sailed from the Red Sea, and appeared
three years later at the Pillars of Hercules—our
Strait of Gibraltar—having circumnavigated the
African continent. It is the fact, however, that
about the middle of the fifteenth century nothing
was known—in Europe at least—of the African
coast-line beyond Cape Bojador on the west side, or
Cape Guardafui on the east. From Morocco round
the Cape of Good Hope to the entrance of the Red
Sea was a complete *terra incognita*. It was the Portuguese who took up the quest for a sea-passage to
India, and after eighty years of glorious effort they
carried their flag triumphantly to the goal. The

man to whom, above all others, Europe is indebted
for the discovery of the pathway to the East, and for
the revival of modern commercial enterprise, is Prince
Henry of Portugal, named the Navigator, son of
King John I. of "good memory."   Prince Henry had
gained renown by fighting the Moors in Africa, and
was high in the counsels of his own country; but it
is as the first great promoter of the spirit of maritime discovery that he has won imperishable fame.
His motives were partly patriotic, he wished to see
his countrymen outstrip the Genoese and Venetians
in the race to the markets of the East; but he had
also an ardent and unquenchable love of knowledge
for its own sake.   "Until his day," says Mr. Major
of the British Museum, in his admirable Life of the
hero, " the pathways of the human race had been the
mountain, the river, and the plain, the strait, the lake,
the inland sea; but he it was who first conceived the
thought of opening up a road through the unexplored
ocean—a road replete with danger, but abundant in
promise."

It was in the year 1415 that Prince Henry
sent out his first expedition to trace the African
coast.   From that date till his death in 1460 no year
passed in which he did not send forth a vessel—often
more than one—to follow up the quest and push a
little further to the southward.   Abandoning the
royal court, and taking up his residence on the bare
and storm-swept promontory of Sagres, the extreme
south-western corner of Europe, he devoted himself
heart and soul to his work.   Never was a purpose

followed up with such heroic and unflinching resolution, and never has success been more magnificent and far-reaching in its results. For years he had to fight against failure and ridicule, and not till 1435 was Cape Bojador rounded; and twenty years more elapsed ere the Venetian Cadamosto doubled Cape de Verd and sighted the mouth of the Gambia. But by years of unwearying endeavour Prince Henry at length succeeded in breathing his spirit into Europe. He fashioned a race of intrepid seamen, and inspired not his countrymen alone but other nations with the passion for adventure and the thirst for new knowledge. The Portuguese explorers, taught and encouraged by experience, took wider flights. No longer crawling along the coasts of the desert, exposed to the fiery breath of the Sahara and the countless dangers from shoals, currents, and storms, and the inveterate hostility of the barbarous Moors, they ventured boldly into mid-ocean. Within little more than a quarter of a century after Prince Henry's death, Diego Cam had discovered the mouth of the Congo, and traced the African coast almost to the Orange River; Bartholomew Diaz had doubled that "Cape of Storms" which succeeding voyagers rechristened "of Good Hope;" and twelve years later Vasco da Gama had fulfilled the long-delayed hope of accomplishing the sea-passage to India. In another direction, but originating in the same impulse, Columbus had discovered a new world in the west; and a few years later Australia had been visited, and Magellan's battered vessel and the remnants of his crew arrived at

San Lucar, having completed the circumnavigation of the world. All this, as Mr. Major points out, had been the work of "one century of continuous and connected discovery," and it may all be traced back to the far-seeing thought and indomitable will of one man.

There are two points especially worthy of notice in the early history of the Portuguese exploration of Africa. One of these is the discovery of the mouth of the Senegal, the first permanent stream of any consequence met with on the southward voyaging. Prince Henry and the other geographical experts of his day considered it to be the "western outlet of the Nile;" and their conclusion was not so utterly ridiculous and far from the mark as appears to us at first sight. If it has no connection with the Nile system, it belongs at least to the same class of streams, utterly distinct from those of the desert, and draws its waters from the same region of regular and abundant rainfall. It was here, in fact, where Europe first set eyes on that moist, luxuriant, intertropical Africa which is still being unfolded before it, and which at that time was so completely at variance with preconceived ideas. Here, too, the African elephant was again seen in its wild state—a glorious promise of the sport that lay in store for the hunter of a later era. Cadamosto was wonderfully struck with the sudden change, not only in the country, but in the inhabitants. "On the south side of the river the people were very black, stout, and well made, and the country verdant, woody, and fertile; while on the north side the men were thin, tawny, and short, and the country dry and sterile." The races of mixed Moorish and Arab blood and Mohammedan religion were about to be left behind, and acquaintance made for the first time as a people—individual specimens had of course been seen scattered throughout the eastern countries—with the Negro. In the quaint language of these old voyagers it was the borderland of the Tawny Moors and the Black Moors (" black-a-moors").

Unhappily the wrongs of the negro began with his first contact with Europeans. The first idea that occurred to the Portuguese mariners on seeing this new black race was to capture specimens and bring them home. The practice, there can be little question, was the first beginnings of the west coast slave-trade. All the maritime nations of Europe fastened themselves like leeches on the side of Africa and sucked her life-blood, and none more greedily, as we should blush to remember, than the English. Millions literally of her children were carried off to the plantations of Brazil, the West Indies, the Spanish Main, and the British Colonies; and as many more died in mid-passage. Slavery, which may be said to have been the staple trade of Africa during three centuries, was fatal to that spirit of research and discovery which the " Navigator" had called into life. The slaver cared not, because he dared not, to venture far from the rendezvous in the lagoon or the barracoons on the river where his victims were collected; and he did all in his power to hide his haunts

and close the doors of ingress to all who would be
likely to interfere with his gains. The slave-trade,
more than any impediments offered by nature, has
stood chiefly in the way of the opening up of the
African continent; and it was not until it received
its death-blow early in the present century that
explorers began to make their way into the interior,
and map out its blank spaces with magnificent lakes
and rivers.

With the great work done by Caille, Barth,
Richardson, Overweg, Rohlfs, Vogel, Nachtigal,
and other discoverers, along the margin and occasionally through the heart of the great northern
desert, we shall in this place have nothing to say; it
lies quite beyond the region of the great equatorial
lakes. Neither can we enter on the stirring narrative of
the travels of Mungo Park, Landers, Clapperton, and
other investigators of the course of the Niger, or seek
to trace the northward march of that army of colonists,
Dutch and English, who have carried cultivation and
civilization from the Cape Mountain to the limit of
the Kalihari Desert, the southern equivalent of the
Sahara. But between these two sterile tracts lies a
vast expanse of Africa, the exploration of which, if it
does not call forth greater powers of endurance or
more heroic courage, promises at least to yield incom-
parably greater results than can be looked for to the
northward. It is a region whose physical features
are homogeneous and unique and on the grandest
scale, where Nature has been most prodigal in all
her gifts. It contains the reservoirs and upper courses

of the three great African streams—the Nile, the
Congo, and the Zambesi—whose waters afford an
unrivalled chain of lake and river communication,
and on whose banks have been found powerful
states and strange peoples and customs of which the
last generation never dreamed. The roll of travellers who have penetrated into it contains such names
as Livingstone, Speke and Grant, Burton, Baker,
Schweinfurth, Gordon, Cameron, Stanley, Kirk, Van
der Decken, Elton, Keith Johnston, Pinto, and others
of hardly lesser note, some of whom have laid down
their lives in witness of their devotion in the cause
of science; and every one of these names recalls
memories of gigantic difficulties grappled with, of
dangers boldly encountered, of sufferings bravely
borne, of great achievements performed, and nearly
all within the short space of twenty years. Surely
the record of such a work could be made interesting.

Before, however, proceeding to describe the region
of the great equatorial lakes, and to narrate the
experiences of recent explorers, it might be well to
refer to another trophy of research, which seems to
hint that all these are but a modern revelation of
what was known three hundred years ago to the
Portuguese colonists of Angola. In an old chart of
the African continent, published at Rome in 1591,
along with a " Description of the Kingdom of Congo "
by one Duarte Lopez, who had spent nine years in
that country, there is shown, in a wonderfully complete and accurate shape, the system of the equatorial
lakes and the rivers connected with them. We have,

for instance, the Blue Nile, flowing through a " Lago Bareena," in Abyssinia, as the Bahr-el-Azrek does through Lake Dembea. Then the White Nile is seen taking its rise in two great lakes on the equator, which might easily represent the Victoria Nyanza of Speke and Albert Nyanza of Sir S. Baker. Due south of what we will say is the Albert Lake is another great fresh-water sea, the equivalent, in the ancient chart, to Tanganyika ; and this is connected not only with the " Rio Congo," but with the Nile and the Zambesi. We know from Stanley's and Cameron's travels that the Tanganyika sends its surplus water to the Congo, and Livingstone has shown that there is continuous water communication between the latter river and the Zambesi. We are not yet in a position either to affirm or deny that a similar connecting link exists between it and the Nile. In fact, in a rough-and-ready way, this map represents pretty correctly the main features of the Lake Region as revealed by the investigations of the last few years; while in regard to other particulars in it, our knowledge is not yet so far extended that we can put our finger on them and say that they do not represent facts. Does the delineation of these remarkable-looking lakes and interlinked river-systems represent a bold and happy guess on the part of the sixteenth century chartographer ? or does it preserve a record of facts, familiar in his day, that afterwards fell into oblivion ? Ere the slave-trade had put its ban of hatred between the coast-dweller and the inhabitant of the interior, when Portuguese influence was predominant in Abyssinia, and a native Christian kingdom of Congo sent missions to the Pope, it is quite conceivable that the true facts concerning the Nile and Congo sources may have come to light. This scrap, then, dug from among the rubbish of the Vatican Library, may possibly be the sole relic now extant of a race of medieval explorers, the fame of whose adventures has "fallen dumb," and whose labours have had to be done over again.

Part First.—The Nile.

CHAPTER I.

THE SECRET OF THE NILE.

" When geographers on Afric maps
With savage pictures filled the gaps,
O'er uninhabitable downs
Placed elephants instead of towns."
SWIFT.

OME thirty years ago the modern world was startled and gratified with its first glimpse at the Lake Region of equatorial Africa. Pigafetta's map was still covered with the thick dust of centuries; it had to be "discovered" like the lakes themselves. Or, if any one in these days had glanced at its wild complication of inland seas and lake-like rivers, he would have been vastly amused. The more he knew, or thought he knew, of geography, the louder he would have laughed. The maps which our fathers used at school showed as a rule a great blank occupying the interior of Africa, from the Abyssinian mountains to the Orange River, and from the coast ranges on the west side to the corresponding face of the table-land

on the east. No geographer had soiled the pure white expanse with his lines and figures; it was the happy hunting-grounds of conjecture and fancy. The Zambesi and the mighty Congo itself were represented as short stumps of rivers, with perhaps a dotted prolongation into the interior, drawn according to the geographer's fancy. A couple of native traders—the Pombeiros—had, indeed, early in the present century, passed from the Portuguese colony of Angola to the eastern side of the continent, and told how, on their journey, they had crossed a hundred rivers, visited the courts of powerful negro kings, and traversed countries where the inhabitants had made considerable progress in arts and industry. Their story, like that of other pioneers, was generally discredited, and themselves and their stores of information treated with contemptuous neglect.

But about thirty years ago authentic intelligence began to be received of the existence of great lakes in the interior. On the 1st of August 1849 Livingstone, Oswell, and Murray, after weary marching across the Kalihari Desert, stood on the margin of Lake Ngami, the most southerly and the first discovered of the great chain of equatorial lakes. As we shall often have occasion to notice, there is no sight so animating and at the same time so tantalizing to the traveller through unknown countries as the sudden glimpse of a grand expanse of water stretching away to the horizon. He expected to find dry land, and, lo! an apparently illimitable sea bars his further journey, and warns him that he must return. But he has made a discovery worth that of scores of nameless rivers and unpronounceable tribes. The fancy is excited with the prospect of vague and almost limitless possibilities, and speculation and conjecture become violently active. The discoverer is drawn back to complete his work, and a score of others plunge into the unexplored to share in his fame.

From the discovery of Ngami probably may be dated the revival of modern curiosity in the secrets of the African continent. Rumours were rife in the Portuguese colonies of the existence of a large lake to the north of the Zambesi, known as Maravi, or Nyassa. Its outflow was unknown, and a favourite theory was that it belonged to the system of the Nile, and was part of a long chain of reservoirs from which the river of Egypt drew its exhaustless store of water. Only the Nile, said these speculators, who, like all their contemporaries, had formed a most inadequate idea of the volume and character of the other two great streams of Central Africa, was worthy of such a magnificent gathering-ground. There were others who believed they confuted this view by pointing to the "Mountains of the Moon." This was a venerable geographical fiction which, like a huge caterpillar, had sprawled for centuries across the breadth of Africa, somewhere about the neighbourhood of the equator. Nobody had penetrated their mysterious recesses, or could even say he had sighted their peaks on the horizon, but there lay the "fountains of the Nile," according to Ptolemy and other ancient geographers, whose authority on this point, if it could be questioned, at least could not be contradicted. There is reason to believe that in this story of the Nile fountains, first told by Herodotus, on the authority of the "Secretary of Minerva at Sais," survives a venerable practical joke played by a party of facetious Egyptian priests on the geographer more than two thousand three hundred years ago. This worthy but credulous old Greek gentleman visited the land of the Pharaohs, then a great seat of learning and art, and the scholarly ecclesiastics naturally paid their distinguished visitor a good deal of attention, pointing out to him with just national pride the vast monuments of Egyptian industry and ingenuity, whose ruins are still the astonishment of the world. At length the stranger put a "poser." "Whence comes this great flood that issues from the desert where there is neither rainfall nor running stream except itself? and what is the secret of that periodical rise in its waters by which Egypt is kept continually green and fertile?" The Egyptian priests of 450 B.C. could no more answer than could the Egyptians of last generation; but they had observed how ready their visitor was to produce his tablets, and the air of complete sincerity with which he jotted down in them the most astounding particulars; so, winking slyly to one another, they told him the cock-and-bull story of the "two conical hills, named Crophi and Mophi," midway between which were "the unfathomable fountains of the Nile, half the water running northward into Egypt, and half

southward into Ethiopia." No doubt when his back
was turned the rogues poked one another in the ribs
—if that was one of the fashions in which an ancient
Egyptian testified his delight in the arts of deceit—
and chuckled at the manner in which the representative of this new-fangled Greek culture and civilization
had been befooled. It is only justice to Herodotus
to say, however, that he seems more than half to
suspect that his informants were amusing themselves
at his expense.

This piece of ancient Egyptian pleasantry represents the only positive statement which we possessed regarding the sources of the White Nile
down to 1861, when Speke and Grant coming
from the south, and Baker following the valley
of the river towards the equator, almost simultaneously solved the mystery of its flow. The story
too has its tragic side; for, as we shall see, poor
Livingstone, pinning his faith resolutely by Herodotus, and believing that he had discovered the
veritable fountains of the Nile and Mountains of the
Moon far away to the south in the water-shed between
the Congo and Zambesi, turned his back on the
glimpse of home and country which the sight of
Stanley afforded him, and followed this Will-o'-the-
wisp into the swamps of the Bangweolo, to meet his
lonely and lingering death. In Ptolemy's time, six
hundred years after Herodotus, some genuine information regarding the Nile sources must have filtered
through to Egypt; for he tells us that the great river
takes its rise, some ten degrees south of the equator,

in many streams that converge into two lakes, situated east and west of each other, from which issue two rivers that join and form the Nile.

'The unravelling of the problem of the Nile has been a favourite dream of the conquerors of Egypt since and probably long before Homer sang of its "heaven-descended stream," whose mythical head-waters were a favourite haunt of Jove himself when the king of the celestials wished to revel and disport himself in absolute seclusion from the children of men. In the days especially when cultivation and a settled population extended far to the south of their present limits, and a powerful state flourished at Meroë, near the junction of the White and Blue Niles, the tramp of armed hosts on the march for the mythical "fountains" has often resounded deep into the African interior. Sesostris, the first king who patronized map-making, made attempts to discover these springs. Alexander of Macedon, Cambyses the Persian, and the Roman Cæsars were inspired with the same wish. We are told by Lucan that Julius Cæsar said he would give up civil war could he but look on the sources of the Nile; and Nero despatched a party of centurions, who returned with wonderful stories of cataracts and marshes that compelled them to return. The measure of success indeed that attended these renowned warriors and hectoring heroes was poor in proportion to the vast means they set in motion to gain it. Their first motive was plunder and conquest, and the long trains of laden camels and captives that followed

their returning march carried away few spoils of
science. The idea of the solitary explorer, with his
life in his hand and goodwill towards man in his
heart, encountering all the perils and privations of
African travel for pure love of knowledge, is wholly
a modern conception; and it is with modern discovery
we have to deal.

Something must be said, however, of one remarkable political personage, who strangely combined the practice of the Oriental despot with the
theories of the modern man of science, and to whom,
perhaps, more than to any other man we are chiefly
indebted for the complete solution of the mystery of
the Nile. This is Ismail Pasha, the ex-viceroy of
Egypt. Now that he has fallen hopelessly from his
high estate, and has himself become a wanderer and
an exile, his great services in the cause of discovery
and international commerce may be heartily acknowledged. His career has been a failure, relieved by brilliant flashes of success. If he has deserved ill of his
people, to whom he owed his first duty, he has deserved nobly of science. He has overwhelmed Egypt
with debt, and ground its people into the dust with
burdens heavier than they could bear; but he introduced to them the light of Western knowledge; he
built the Suez Canal, and he sought out and an-
nexed the sources of the Nile. For twenty years an
army of European pioneers and explorers in the khe-
dive's pay or under his protection have been working
their way southward, mapping out lakes and rivers,
founding settlements, capturing slave-gangs, until now

KOROSKO, THE STARTING-PLACE FOR THE DESERT.

Page 32.

the whole extent of the Nile valley, from the equator
to the Mediterranean, owns the sway of Egypt,
and is open to the influences of commerce and civilization.   Every one has heard of the series of cataracts that obstruct the navigation of the river
between Assouan in Upper Egypt and Khartoum
in the Soudan.   Among the many schemes undertaken by Ismail Pasha in pursuance of his grand
idea of making Egypt coextensive with the Nile
was that of constructing a "ship incline" over the
First Cataract, and running a line of railway from
Wady Halfa, near the Second Cataract, to Khartoum,
and ultimately, perhaps, to the great lakes.   The
great work, we believe, has actually been begun;
but considering the financial condition of Egypt it is
not likely that any one will be privileged, during the
present generation, to travel express in a comfortable
railway carriage from Cairo to the margin of the
Victoria Nyanza!

On the journey we are about to take we must, like
the first pioneers, be content with a much more slow
and laborious method of travelling, over a route still
beset with numberless dangers.   And on the very
threshold we meet with the most formidable obstacle
of all to an advance into the interior of Africa from
the side of Egypt or the Red Sea—the great Nubian
Desert.   This dreary tract we must cross, otherwise
we can have no adequate idea of the hardships of the
explorer's life, the difficulties and discouragements he
meets with at the very outset, and the surprising contrast between his experiences in the earlier and in the

(655)   3

later stages of his progress. His voyage up the Nile,
under the ever clear and brilliant sky of Egypt, past
the silent shapes of the temples, the sphinxes, the
pyramids, and other gigantic monuments of a great
past, and surrounded by the sights and sounds of
Oriental life, has been a holiday trip to the traveller
bound lakewards. When he places his foot on the
desert sand, and transfers his guns, his tent, and
other *impedimenta* of travel from the river-boat to
the back of the "ship of the desert" which is to convey him across the Great Bend of the Nile from
Korosko to Abu Hammed, the stern reality of his
task begins. The first day's sun, reflected with overpowering force from the fantastic cliffs and flinty
sand of the Korosko Desert, probably burns out of
him any romance that he may have entertained in
connection with Nubian travel; before the nearest
halting-place is reached, the early delightful sense of
the novelty of riding on camel-back has given place
to a hearty detestation of the uneasy motion, the slow
progress, and the abominable temper of that over-
landed brute. Soon you are glad to abandon
travel in the full blaze of day, with its blistering
glare from rock and sand, the pitiless sun overhead,
and the furnace-like breath of the desert air, and
you march at night, when the earth is growing cool
again, under the great stars. Here and there, as you
descend into the bed of a "wady," or dry water-course,
the eye is relieved for an instant by a patch of green
verdure, a frightened gazelle dashes away to the
shelter of the nearest sand-hills, or a glimpse is caught

SIR SAMUEL AND LADY BAKER ON THE MARCH.

Page 37.

of a naked Arab youth tending his flock of goats ; for
even the desert is not entirely void of plant and animal life, though every living thing seems to partake
of the arid nature and to bear the dusty colours of
the surrounding waste.   Even rain is not altogether
unknown, and it is looked for at least once every
winter season, though sometimes four years will pass
without a fall.

At these times the clouds that have drifted up
from the distant Indian Ocean may be seen pitching
their black tents about the summits of the mountain
ridges that divide the Nile Valley from the Red Sea.
The nomad Arab tribes, the only inhabitants of these
thirsty hills, watch them with breathless hope.   A
north wind may blow during the night and drift
them back whence they came.   More likely they
burst in thunderstorm—the whole of the storms of a
season compressed into one furious onslaught of lightning and rain.   The dry wadies of yesterday are
roaring torrents by morning, bearing down to the
Nile a tribute of water for one day in the year at
least.   For one day also, or perhaps for some weeks,
the earth and air are swept of their impurities, and
the face of the desert begins to look fresh and verdant,
as grass and plants spring up rapidly on every hand ;
but then again the drought and the heat return, and
nature withers more rapidly than it sprang to life.
There are spots, however, well known to the Arab
shepherd and camel-driver, where there are running
water and green turf all the year round, or where,
sheltered perhaps by the naked rocks of some deep

ravine, a little oasis of palm and tamarisk trees is to
be found. These are the halting-places on the march
—the stepping-stones by means of which alone this
howling wilderness may be crossed. Sometimes the
wells fail, or are poisoned, or a predatory band occupies the springs; and then the unfortunate traveller
has to face the peril of death from thirst or exhaustion as the fainting caravan is hurried forward to the
next halting-place. In any case he is fervently
thankful when the shining waters of the Nile come
again into sight at Abu Hammed, and this doleful
stage of his desert wandering is at a close.

But the "secret of the Nile" seems, if possible,
further from solution than ever; and the stream
whose shores he now follows for many weary marches
is even a more mysterious phenomenon in Upper
Nubia than it is as it flows under the walls of Cairo.
In the twelve hundred miles of its lower course the
Nile receives no tributary either on the right hand or
on the left. It may be traced like a ribbon of silver
with a narrow fringe of green, winding in great folds
through a hot and thirsty desert, and under the full
blaze of a sun that drinks its waters but returns nothing
to it in the shape of rain; and man also exacts a heavy
tribute from it for the irrigation of the soil. It is not
till we reach the mouth of the Atbara—the Bahr-el-
Azwab or Black Nile—that some light begins to
break in as to the sources of this exhaustless store of
water. Even the Atbara though in some respects
the most important of the Nile tributaries, is but a
dry river-bed during a great part of the year. Its

sources are away to the left, in the Abyssinian mountains, whose great buttresses now begin to cut the
eastern horizon.   There also are a " Lake Region "
and " Nile sources," the discovery of which by Bruce
about a century ago made a great talk in the world.
But we must not step aside to climb that stupendous
wall, or look upon the wonders beyond, great though
the temptations are.   Abyssinia is a country so unique
in its physical features, its social life, its history, its
religion, and its archæological remains, that it is small
wonder that Bruce's account of his sojourn there was
at first received with incredulity.   The thorough
trustworthiness of his narrative has been established
by the brothers D'Abbadie, Dr. Beke, De Cosson, and
other recent explorers; and James Bruce — " the
greatest among us all," as Dr. Livingstone declares—
has taken his proper place as one of the most accurate
of observers, as well as most intrepid of travellers.

It was Sir Samuel Baker, however, on his first journey up the Nile in the summer of 1861, who first
adequately pointed out the part played by the Abyssinian streams in the phenomena of the Nile—a
part scarcely, if any, inferior to that of the equatorial
lakes themselves.   Sir Samuel turned aside from
his southward route and followed the dry bed of the
Atbara, partly to enjoy the hunting of the " big
game " — the elephant, rhinoceros, hippopotamus,
giraffe, and lion—that abound in the thick jungles
covering the lower slopes of these hills, and partly to
watch the great annual flooding of the Nile tributaries.   The " Black Nile " was simply a vast furrow

thirty feet in depth and from four hundred yards to
half a mile in breadth, ploughed through the heart
of the desert, its edges marked by a thin growth of
leafless mimosas and dome palms. The only trace of
water was here and there a rush-fringed pool which
the impetuous torrent had hollowed out in the sudden
bends in the river's course, and where disported
themselves hippopotami, crocodiles, and immense
turtles, that had long ago adjusted their relations on
a friendly footing on the discovery that none of
them could do harm to the others. On the 23rd of
June, the simoom was blowing with overpowering
force: the heat was furnace-like, and the tents of the
travellers were covered with several inches of drifted
sand. Above, in the Abyssinian mountains, however,
the lightnings were playing and the rains were falling as if the windows of heaven had been opened.
The monsoon had set in; the rising streams were
choking their narrow channels in their frantic rush
to the lowlands, and were tearing away huge masses
of the rich dark soil, to be spread a month hence over
the flat plains of Egypt. The party encamped on the
Atbara heard through the night a sound as if of distant thunder: but it was "the roar of the approaching water." The traveller describes the scene best
in his own words :—

"On the morning of the 24th of June I stood on
the banks of the noble Atbara river at break of day.
Wonder of the desert! Yesterday there was a barren
sheet of glaring sand, with a fringe of withered bush
and trees upon its borders that cut the yellow ex-

SCENE ON THE ATBARA.

Page 34.

panse of desert. For days we had journeyed along the exhausted bed. All nature, even in nature's poverty, was most poor: no bush could boast a leaf, no tree could throw a shade; crisp gums crackled upon the stems of the mimosas—the sap dried upon the burst bark, sprung with the withering heat of the simoom. In one night there was a mysterious change —wonders of the mighty Nile! An army of water was hastening to the wasted river. There was no drop of rain, no thunder-cloud on the horizon to give hope—all had been dry and sultry; dust and desolation yesterday, to-day a magnificent stream, five hundred yards in width and from fifteen to twenty feet in depth, flowed through the dreary desert! Bamboos and reeds, with trash of all kinds, hurry along the muddy waters. Where are all the crowded inhabitants of the pool? The prison doors are open, the prisoners released, and rejoicing in the mighty stream of the Atbara."

We turn our back reluctantly on this majestic mountain mass, which, with its head capped with snow and its feet in the dust of the desert, stretches upwards through so many zones, and performs such wonderful functions. We have the clue to one part of the Nile mystery—its great periodical inundations, the source of its fertilizing slime. The Bahr-el-Azrek, the Blue Nile of Bruce, contributes, like the Atbara, though in a secondary degree, to the flood of the river and the fertility of Egypt, with this difference, that it brings down some water all the year round. At Khartoum we reach the junction between the

Blue and the White Nile, the frontier also of two
strongly-contrasted physical regions, and the dividing
line between barbarism and savagery. The secret
that has still to be unveiled is the source of that unfailing flow of water which, resisting the influences
of absorption, evaporation, and irrigation, carries a
life-giving stream through the heart of Egypt at all
seasons of the year.

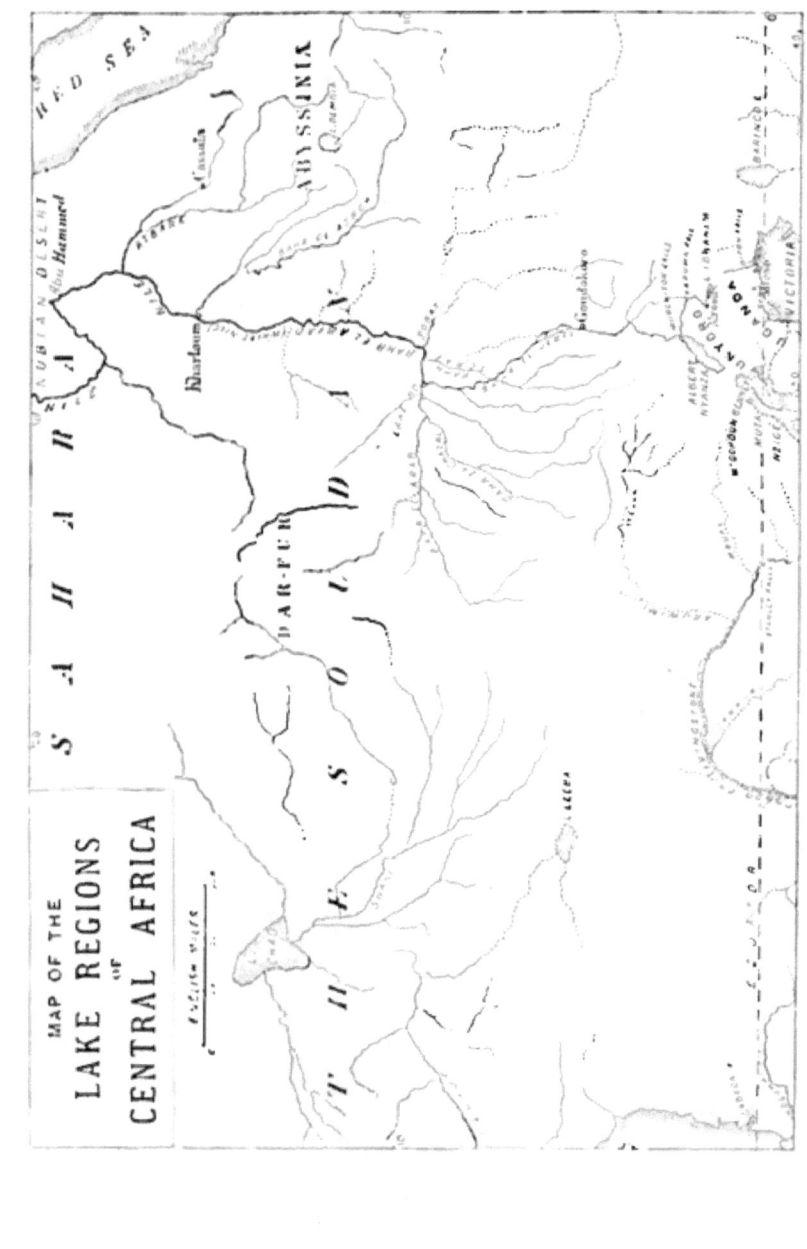

MAP OF THE
LAKE REGIONS
OF
CENTRAL AFRICA

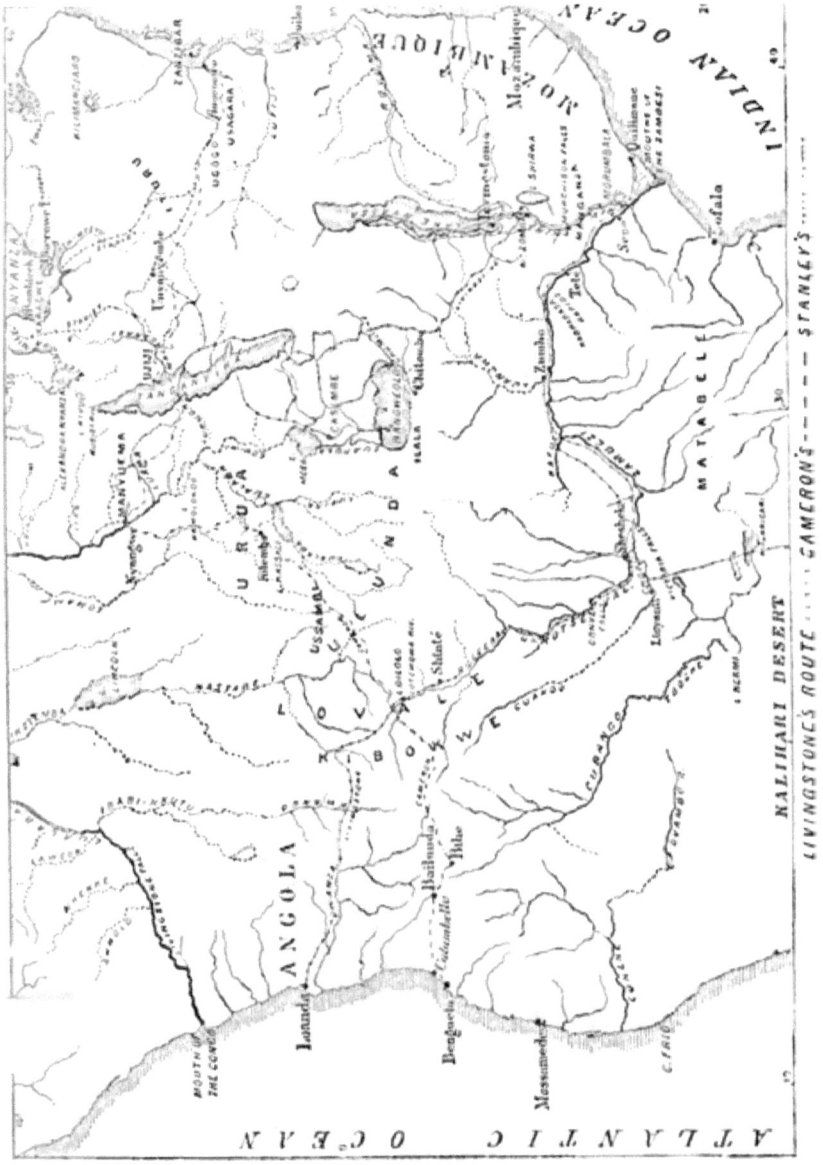

CHAPTER II.

THE WHITE NILE AND THE ALBERT NYANZA.

EITHER civilization nor savagedom has
much credit by their border-city. Khar-
toum has ingrafted all the vices of the
one state of society on the squalor and
misery of the other. A traveller sums up its attractions by the remark that "a more miserable, filthy,
and unhealthy spot can hardly be imagined;" and
other visitors have heartily endorsed the opinion.
Nevertheless it is an interesting place. Here, up to
a comparatively recent date, was the "Threshold of
the Unknown." It has been the starting-point of
almost numberless Nile expeditions, since the days
perhaps of the Pharaohs. Mehemet Ali, the first
viceroy of Egypt, and grandfather of Ismail Pasha,
got a little way to the south of it in his conquest of
the Soudan in 1839. He found the climate so unhealthy that he established a penal settlement at
Fazougli, a little distance up the White Nile, banish-
ment to which was regarded as equivalent to sen-

tence of death. At the time of Linant's expedition
nothing was known beyond the fourteenth degree
of north latitude, or about a hundred miles south
of Khartoum. The wilderness of fever-stricken
marshes that line the White Nile long baffled the
attempts of the most determined explorers to penetrate to the southward. At length "dry land" was
reached again at Gondokoro, only five degrees from
the equator. It in turn became an advanced position of Egyptian authority, a centre of mission
enterprise, a half-way house where the traveller
rested and equipped himself for new discoveries.
From the base of Gondokoro, Petherick pursued his
researches into the condition of the negro races of
the Upper Nile; the Italian traveller, Miani, penetrated far towards the south-west, into the countries
occupied by the Nyam-Nyam tribes, that singular
region of dwarfs and cannibals; and Dr. Schweinfurth, Colonel Long, and Mdlle. Tinné followed up
the search with magnificent results. Mdlle. Tinné,
a brave Dutch lady, deserves special notice as having
been perhaps the first European woman who encountered the terrible hardships and perils of the
explorer's life in the cause of African discovery.
She is far, however, from being the last. The wives
of two of the greatest pioneers in the work—Mrs.
Livingstone and Lady Baker—accompanied with a
noble-minded resolution the steps of their husbands,
the one along the banks of the Zambesi, and the
other on the White Nile. Mdlle. Tinné and Mrs.
Livingstone paid with their lives for their devotion,

MADEMOISELLE TINNE.

Page 38.

and are buried by the streams from whose waters they helped to raise the veil. Lady Baker has been more fortunate. Only a girl of seventeen when she rode by her husband's side from Gondokoro, she has lived to return to Europe from the inmost heart of Africa, and her name will be associated indissolubly with the two great events of recent African history—the discovery of the great lakes and the suppression of the slave traffic.

For unfortunately explorers and missionaries were not the only strangers who were attracted to this region of the White Nile. It has long been one of the great man-hunting grounds of Africa. The Egyptian conquest of the Soudan rather gave a stimulus to the trade than otherwise. The traffic was in the heyday of its prosperity as the European travellers were struggling to reach the equatorial lakes, and the pages of their journals reveal its horrors in all their hideous nakedness. Arab traders were the chief actors in these enterprises; but a motley crew of other nations, including—with shame it must be said—some of white race, took a share in them; and they were under the scarcely-disguised patronage, and very largely for the profit, of the Egyptian authorities at Khartoum and elsewhere. Khartoum marks pretty exactly the limit of the area occupied by the Arab race in this direction, and also of the main influence of the Mussulman religion. Beyond it we have the negro and the pagan. Fanaticism and race hatred, therefore, helped to inflame the evil passions which the slave trade invariably arouses. The business of the miscreants engaged in this detestable work was simply kidnapping and murder. The trade of the White Nile was purely slave-hunting. The trifling traffic in ivory and gums was a mere deception and sham, intended to cover the operations of the slaver. A marauding expedition would be openly fitted out at Khartoum, composed of some of the most atrocious ruffians in Africa and south-western Asia, with the scum of a few European cities. Their favourite mode of going to work was to take advantage of one of those wars which are constantly being waged between the tribes of Central Africa. If a war were not going on in the quarter which the slave-hunters had marked out for their raid, a quarrel was purposely fomented—at no time a difficult task in Africa. At dead of night the marauders with their black allies would steal down upon the doomed village. At a signal the huts are fired over the heads of the sleeping inmates, a volley of musketry is poured in, and the gang of desperadoes spring upon their victims. A scene of wild confusion and massacre follows, until all resistance has been relentlessly put down, and then the slave-catcher counts over and secures his human spoils. This is the first act of the bloody drama. Most probably, if the kidnappers think they have not made a large enough "haul," they pick a quarrel with their allies, who are in their turn shot down, or overpowered, and manacled to their late enemies, are soon floating down the Nile in a slave dhow, on their way to the markets of Egypt or Turkey.

The waste of human life, the stoppage of industry and honest trade, the demoralization of the whole region within reach of the raiders, the detestable cruelties and crimes practised on the helpless captives on the journey down the river, on the caravan route across the desert, or in the stifling dens where they are lodged at the slave depots and markets, represent an enormous total of human misery. The efforts of Baker Pasha, Gordon Pasha, and other lieutenants of the viceroy of Egypt, together with the measures taken by European powers to intercept slave cargoes on the Red Sea and Indian Ocean, have given, it may be hoped, a death-blow to the traffic. So closely is it bound up with all the social and commercial usages of Central Africa that it will linger on for many a day to come, and at the first symptom of relaxed watchfulness it will revive to new life. Again and again it has raised its hateful head in the Upper Nile region; and only the other day Colonel Gordon had to lead a large expedition against a force of some two thousand lawless adventurers who still openly persevered in their piratical enterprises. But for the most part they now pursue obscure paths, and rely more on guile and cunning than on force for securing their prey. The story of the suppression of the White Nile slave trade has still to be told; for Colonel Gordon, the man who has been the chief actor in the work, has a most rare " talent for silence," and has not as yet taken the world into his confidence with regard to his wonderful adventures as " Governor-General of the Soudan "

—a post which he has now resigned. Knight-errant never met with more startling experiences, and certainly never undertook a task of such real and lasting value to the cause of humanity and discovery.

While with the slave trade has been removed the chief impediment to the opening up of the Nile sources, the actual physical difficulties met with have been stupendous. Entering the White Nile, we plunge into a new world—a region whose climate and animal and vegetable life, in brief, whose whole aspect and nature, are totally unlike those of the desert which stretches up to the walls of Khartoum. We are within the zone of regular rainfall, an intermediate region that extends to the margin of the great lakes, where we meet with the equatorial belt of perennial rains. Henceforth we have not only heat but moisture acting upon the face of nature.

One may determine which of the two climates is the more tolerable by considering whether he would prefer to be roasted or stewed. The traveller would find it hard to decide whether the desert or the swamp is the greater bar to his advance. Every mile of progress marks an increase of dampness and of warmth. First of all, we pass through the great mimosa forest, which extends, belt-like, almost across the continent, marking the confines of the Sahara and the Soudan. The reader must not imagine a dense girdle of tall trees and tangled undergrowth, but a park-like country, with wide glades between clumps and lines of thorny shrubbery. The mimosa, or Arabian acacia—the tree

SWAMPS OF THE WHITE NILE.

Page 59.

from which the gum-arabic of commerce is extracted
—has assigned to it the outpost duty in the struggle
between tropical luxuriance and desert drought;
and its lines are extended in "skirmishing order."

By-and-by it gives place to the ambatch, as the
characteristic tree of the Nile. The margin of the
river becomes marshy and reedy. The water encroaches on the land, and the land on the water.
The muddy stream rolls lazily between high walls of
rank vegetation, and bearing islands of intertwisted
leaves, roots, and stems on its bosom. It breaks up
into tortuous channels that seem to lead nowhere
and everywhere. A nearly vertical sun shines down
on the voyager as he slowly toils up-stream; scarcely
a breath of wind is stirring to blow away the malarious mists that rise from the steaming shores, or to
shake out his drooping sail. Worst plague of all,
the mosquitoes are incredibly active and numerous.
Nothing can ward off their persistent attacks, or
satiate their thirst for blood. Day follows day with
scarcely an event to break the dreary monotony.
Now and then, perhaps, the unwieldy shape of a
hippopotamus comes snorting to the surface, a crocodile shows his vicious jaws, or where the banks are
more solid than elsewhere a buffalo pushes his head
through the reeds to drink. The true river margin
is invisible, except from the boat's mast, over the
heads of the tall papyrus stems with their funereal
plumes. Could we reach it, we would probably be
glad to sheer off again; for of all the growths of this
dismal swamp man is the most repulsive. The

Dinka tribes of the White Nile are among the lowest
in the scale of human beings. Utterly innocent of
clothing, travellers tell us they are equally destitute
of moral qualities. The Shillooks are a finer race
physically, but they are inveterate pirates and murderers; and the traveller, if not himself too strongly
supported to fear molestation, would do wisely to
give their canoes of ambatch a wide berth.

At the entrance of the Sobat a glimpse is
caught of a vista of open water rolling down from
the southern Abyssinian highlands, where, Dr.
Beke tells, the stream runs for seven days' journey
through a forest so dense as completely to exclude
the rays of the sun. Above the Sobat mouth, however, we meet with the greatest of all the obstruc-
tions of the Nile—with what is, in fact, the lowest
of the Nile reservoirs. Here, at the union of the
main stream of the White River with the numerous
channels of the Bahr-el-Ghazal, coming from the
west, and with other affluents on the right bank, has
been formed a vast marsh through which the water
soaks as through a sponge. In the centre is a small
nucleus of a lake—Lake No; but to reach it, or to
emerge from it again, or to thread by any other
track a way through this net-work of blind creeks
and labyrinthine channels, demands inexhaustible
patience and skill. Yet across this Slough of Des-
pond Sir S. Baker managed, in his second Nile
expedition, to cut a canal, through which was towed,
or rather dragged, the first steamer that ever floated
on the head-waters of the great river. If by extraor-

dinary good-luck we escape scathless from the clutches
of the fever and the savages, we step again upon dry
land, with unspeakable thankfulness, at Gondokoro.

Seventeen years ago—probably the description
applies at the present moment, though Egypt has
since made it a military station, and renamed it
Ismailia—Gondokoro was a squalid collection of
grass huts, in the midst of an untrodden wilderness,
and surrounded by barbarous and hostile tribes. It
was the scene, however, of one of the most interesting
episodes in the history of discovery. One evening in
February 1863 a travel-stained caravan, with two
white men at its head, crested the high ground above
the station, and with shouts, waving of flags, and rattle
of musketry, came briskly down the slope. It was
Speke and Grant, thus far on their overland march
from Zanzibar, with the secret of the Nile in their
pockets. On their long tramp they had visited
strange new peoples and countries, and by courage and
tact had escaped unharmed from a multitude of perils.
They had traced the western shore of that vast
reservoir of fresh water which Speke had sighted on
a previous expedition, and had named the Victoria
Nyanza. They had seen the lake discharging its
surplus waters to the northward over the Ripon
Falls, and knew that they had solved the great
geographical puzzle of the day. Lower down, at
the Karuma Falls, they were compelled to leave
the stream, which they now knew to be the Nile,
and crossing to the right bank, they made straight
across country to Gondokoro. Here they came in

sight of the farthest outpost of Egyptian exploration,
and again looked upon the river that was to bear
them down to the Mediterranean.

By a curious coincidence, the first Englishman
who had penetrated so far to the southward was at
that moment in Gondokoro. Samuel Baker and his
wife were interrupted in their preparations for their
journey to the Nile sources by the noise of the
approaching party, and they rode out to see what
all the hubbub meant. Four people from a distant nook of Europe met in the heart of Africa;
and as they clasped hands, the hoary secret of the
Nile was unriddled! All of them had numberless
difficulties before as well as behind them; but their
hearts were undismayed, and swelled only with
pride at what had been accomplished for science and
for their native land. The travellers from Zanzibar
bore the marks of their long journey—"battered and
torn, but sound and seaworthy." "Speke," Baker
tells us, "appeared the more worn of the two; he
was excessively lean, but in reality in good tough
condition. He had walked the whole way from
Zanzibar, never having once ridden during the
wearying march. Grant was in honourable rags,
his bare knees projecting through the remnants of
trousers that were an exhibition of rough industry
in tailor-work. He was looking tired and feverish,
but both men had a fire in the eye that showed the
spirit that had led them through." The first greetings over, Baker's earliest question was, Was there
no leaf of the laurel reserved for him? Yes; there

PREPARATIONS FOR A START.

was. Below the Karuma Falls, Speke and Grant
had been informed, the stream from the Victoria
Nyanza fell into, and almost immediately emerged
again from, another lake, the Luta Nzigé, which
must therefore be the ultimate reservoir of the Nile
waters. No European had ever seen this basin, or
even heard of it before; and Baker determined that
this should be his share of the prize.

A new class of obstacles and risks, however, meet
us when we undertake, as we must do here, a land
journey in intertropical Africa. There is no longer,
as in the desert, the peril of death from thirst or
starvation; for the country abounds in game, and
our course does not throughout lie through interminable swamp, as in the river navigation. But from the
very beginning we are beset with hindrances and an-
noyances small and great. An army of porters must
be got together,—Stanley numbered his by the thousand,—drilled, and fed. Like other Africans, they
are children of impulse, credulous, suspicious, often
lying, cowardly, and treacherous. On the slightest
provocation they are seized with panic, and desert;
or they take advantage of relaxed discipline, and
mutiny. The leader must be possessed of inexhaustible good-humour, and at the same time be
able to prove, when occasion requires, that he is a
stern master. A dove-like demeanour will hardly
suit the African explorer; he must be wise as a
serpent and watchful as a hawk. When at length a
start is made, difficulties accumulate at every step.
In a country where rain falls for ten or eleven

months in the year, under a vertical sun, the growth
of vegetation is amazing. In the dry season the
grass and shrubs are burned far and wide ; but after
a few weeks' rain the new plant-life starts up with
incredible quickness. The country is covered with
an impenetrable jungle of grass, reeds, and bamboos.
A thick undergrowth starts up below the shade of
the forest trees ; the great stems of the pandanus,
the banana, and the baobab are covered to their tops
with a feathery growth of parasitic ferns and orchids,
and festooned with the tough branches of the wild vine
and the liana, and other twining and creeping plants.
The rivers are at their highest mark, and the marshes
are profound and impassable. The native villages
are almost smothered under the dank luxuriance of
plant-life, and lions and other beasts of prey can
creep up unseen to the very doors of the huts. The
whole country, in short, becomes a tangled brake,
with only here and there an open space, or a rough
track marking where the heavy body of an elephant,
a rhinoceros, or a buffalo has crushed a way through
the high grass. The fact that there is "a lion in the
way"—much more an elephant—is an incentive to
the traveller to push on.

But there are other and worse enemies, whom
he cannot remove from his path by means of his
rifle. Where, as is the case between Gondokoro and
the lakes, the country ahead has been raided by
the slave-hunters, he may count on every stranger
being regarded as an enemy. Or a native war may
be in progress, and on peril of his expedition being

ruined, he must take care not to identify himself
with either belligerent. He must double back, wait,
push on in whatever direction he sees an opening.
The African explorer may not follow what road he
chooses, but only what he can, and that often is to
retrace his steps; sometimes, alas! even the backward path is not open for him, and his grave, if he
has a grave, is dug in the wilderness.

It was through such impediments as these—
which after all are only the lot of every traveller
in tropical Africa—that Baker and his wife at
length reached the Victoria Nile, near the locality
where Speke and Grant had lately crossed it. Before reaching the unknown lake they must pass
through the territory of one of the "Great Powers"
in these parts, Kamrasi M'Kamma, whose kingdom,
Unyoro, occupies the greater part of the country
between the Victoria and Luta Nzigé lakes. And
having on our circuitous way to these great fresh-
water seas glanced at some of the chief drawbacks
to the excitement and romance of the discoverer's
life in Central Africa, something may be said at
this place also of negro kings. They are the greatest
nuisances in Africa, not even excepting the mosquitoes, whom they nearly equal in numbers and
often surpass in ferocity. No one can thoroughly
understand "what hell it is in suing long to bide"
who has not been compelled to pay court to a
black potentate of Equatorial Africa. But this is a
duty which the unfortunate explorer is compelled to
perform at every stage of his journey. The faults

of the humble negro we can forgive. They are
many, but not so numerous as his wrongs; and his
careless good-humour and light-heartedness are
greater than either. But the faults of the average
African king,—there are exceptions to the rule
even here,—are such that human nature cannot
tolerate. As densely ignorant as the meanest of his
subjects, he is complete master of their lives and
property. His cruelty, rapacity, sensuality, whatever bad qualities there are in him, have been
steadily nourished from infancy upwards; and in
virtue of his "little brief authority," he plays such
ridiculous and abominable antics under heaven that
it is not strange to find his white visitors losing all
patience. In his own eyes he is a demi-god; while
his guests see him as a great, hulking, evil-smelling
savage, plastered with grease, clay, and cow-dung,
his palace a reed hut into which you must crawl on
all fours, and his royal robes a scanty blanket of
mat or wild-beast skin. And yet compliments and
presents must be paid to this brutal and cowardly
despot, and precious time wasted in dancing attend-
ance at his silly palavers, or looking on while he
makes a hog of himself by swallowing calabash
after calabash of native beer. Without his "pombe,"
or beer, the African king could hardly exist; and
when it is his royal pleasure to travel, mounted on
the back of one of his courtiers, a large flagon of his
favourite beverage is carried behind him by one of
his wives to refresh his majesty on the road. In
duplicity, cruelty, and rapacity King Kamrasi was

A ROYAL PROGRESS. *Page 50.*

abreast of any black man of his time. Speke and
Grant did not love him for his inordinate and insatiable greed, and the long delays that this caused at
his capital, Mrooli; and Baker had still less reason to
do so. His exactions on that traveller ended in a
demand for an exchange of wives. This was too
much; and the incensed explorer, holding his loaded
revolver within a foot or two of the monarch's chest,
sternly told him that if the insult were repeated he
would shoot the scoundrel dead. This threat had a
due effect, and next day Baker was again on the
march to the lake. And after all it turned out that
it was only a sham Kamrasi, who had been playing
the part of king before the white man; the real
anointed of Unyoro had been skulking among the
attendants, and when an acquaintance is made with
him later, he turns out to be several degrees more
objectionable even than his substitute.

At length, after eighteen days' march through
forest and morass, amid almost continuous rains,
and with his wife for the greater part of the way
borne beside him insensible in a litter—having been
prostrated with sunstroke—the explorer reached the
long-sought-for goal. Ascending a gentle slope, with
little to distinguish it from the other undulations of
the surface, the Luta Nzigé—the Albert Nyanza, as
it was afterwards christened, after an honoured name
in England—burst on his sight, its white waves
breaking on a pebbly beach fifteen hundred feet below.
Far away on the horizon, blue mountains, seven thousand feet in height, could be faintly descried. Their

distance seemed about seventy miles, and the lake
appeared to extend to their very base. Northward
and southward the gleaming expanse of water seemed
limitless. It was a basin worthy of its great func-
tion, as the gathering-place of the head-waters of
the Nile, which issues a full-grown stream from its
northern end. The white strangers who had been
first privileged to look upon this glorious scene lost
no time in hurrying down to the shore of the lake
and bathing their feet in its clear fresh water.
After an adventurous voyage in a frail, native boat,
they reached the lower end of the great reservoir,
where, within a few miles, could be seen the Victoria
Nile entering the lake, and the broad channel
fringed with water-plants where the White Nile
made its exit. Their course lay amid storm and
sunshine; first under beetling precipices that line the
eastern shore of the Albert Nyanza, and down which
jets of water—each a Nile source—could be seen
plunging from a height of one thousand feet into the
lake; and then through a flat waste of reeds, and out
and in among beds of water-plants and floating rafts
of vegetable matter in every stage of growth and
decay.

But the travellers could not wait to examine all
these wonders, or to trace the extent of the Albert
basin. They must be in Gondokoro in a few weeks,
or leave their bones in Central Africa. Turning
into the entrance to the Victoria Nile, and ascending
a few miles, a new marvel greeted them — the
Murchison Falls. "Rounding a corner," says the

THE MURCHISON FALLS.

Page 55.

traveller's record, " a magnificent sight burst upon us.
On either side of the river were beautiful wooded cliffs,
rising abruptly to a height of about three hundred
feet ; rocks were jutting out from the intensely green
foliage; and rushing through a gap that cleft the
rock exactly before us, the river, contracted from a
grand stream, was pent up in a narrow gorge of
scarcely fifty yards in width : roaring furiously
through the rock-bound pass, it plunged in one leap
of about one hundred and twenty feet perpendicular
into a dark abyss below.   The fall of water was now
white, which had a superb effect as it contrasted with
the dark cliffs that walled the river, while the graceful palms of the tropics and wild plantains completed
the beauty of the scene.   This was the greatest waterfall of the Nile."

Since Baker's time, Gordon Pasha and M. Gessi,
in a steamer brought up in pieces from Gondokoro, have navigated the Albert Nyanza, curtailing
it considerably of the fair proportions it showed on
the first maps, and showing that, instead of joining
in at its southern extremity with Tanganyika, it
ends at a distance of about one hundred miles in a
forest of ambatch ; and Colonel Long, M. Linant de
Bellefonds, and others, have traced the whole course
of the Victoria Nile—discovering on their way a new
lake, Ibrahim—as far as the Victoria Nyanza, on
whose mightier waters we must now embark.

CHAPTER III.

A VOYAGE ON THE VICTORIA NYANZA.

"Of most disastrous chances,
Of moving accidents by flood and field,
Of hair-breadth 'scapes."— *Othello.*

IT was from a direction opposite to that in which we have been approaching it that the first sight of the Victoria Nyanza— the queen of African lakes—was caught by a European eye. Its discovery followed closely on that of Tanganyika, and preceded by a few months the finding of Lake Nyassa. The three chief reservoirs of the equatorial rainfall, after remaining hidden since the beginning of history from the sight of all but the barbarous natives of their shores, were revealed to the knowledge of the scientific world within a period of eighteen months. In the summer of 1858, Richard Burton and John Speke, two promising young lieutenants in the Indian army, who had been commissioned by the Royal Geographical Society to search for the supposed Lake Regions in the centre of the African continent, were at Unyanyembe, half-way on their return journey to Zanzibar, after having sighted and

partly explored the great fresh-water reservoir which is now so well known as the Tanganyika. Speke had heard, from Arab and native sources, rumours of a still larger lake that lay far away to the northward; and the idea caught a strong hold upon him that here at last were authentic tidings of the long-sought-for Nile sources. His companion was more sceptical, and decided to remain where he was, arranging and preparing the results of their previous journey, while Speke should pursue alone the new line of exploration.

He started on the 9th of July 1858, and, after three weeks' march over an undulating country intersected by streams flowing to the northward, he came in view, on the 30th of the month, of the head of a deep gulf expanding towards the north. Pursuing his journey along the eastern side of this gulf, he saw, from a height of two hundred feet above its surface, how it opened out into an ocean-like expanse of water, girt in by hill and forest on the right hand and on the left, but stretching away illimitably towards the northward and eastward—"so broad that you could not see across it, and so long that nobody knew its length." "I no longer felt any doubt," he writes, "that the lake at my feet gave birth to that interesting river, the source of which has been the subject of so much speculation and the object of so many explorers."

Unable at the time to pursue his investigations further, he returned to Unyanyembe, and ultimately to England. There his new theory of the Nile sources gave rise to voluminous and sometimes bitter discussion. Two schools of Nile theorists arose; one of which clung to Speke's reading of the problem, while the other held that the new lake was an insignificant detached sheet of water, or, at most, quite a subsidiary reservoir of the great river, whose true head-waters would probably be found in the Tanganyika, if not even farther south. The most powerful supporter of this notion was Speke's old companion, the burly Richard Burton, who has perhaps travelled in and written more about strange countries, and come through more startling experiences, than any man of his generation. Avowedly to substantiate the correctness of his views, Captain Speke was again on the East African Coast in the autumn of 1860, and, in company with Captain Grant, a brother officer, started on one of the most arduous and eventful marches ever undertaken by a discoverer. They followed almost the track which Speke had traversed two years before; but, instead of making for the south end of the lake, they were compelled to strike off towards the left; and, after many adventures and hardships, they found themselves, in the close of 1861, in Karagwe, a country to the west of the Victoria, ruled over by a respectable and mild-tempered old black king named Rumanika. Just as every visitor to Kamrasi has the same story to relate of his rascally greed and brutality, so the explorers whose good fortune has led them to the neighbourhood of Rumanika's head village, have all come

away delighted with his unaffected kindliness and
generous help.

We will meet him, however, further on, and have
to note at present that Speke and Grant were compelled to take up quarters with him for a period that
must have tried the patience of both host and guests,
and that it was not till the end of January 1862 that
our travellers got a first sight of the lake. Then,
keeping well up on the high grounds, they proceeded
on their way northwards, catching only at long intervals a glimpse of the shining waters, until they
arrived at the court of Mtesa, king, or "emperor," as
some will have it, of Uganda. This is, in many
respects, the most interesting personage in Central
Africa, and as important, in his way, to the explorer
as the Victoria Nyanza itself, over which he is the
presiding genius. There is no such unanimity of
opinion regarding Mtesa, as in the case of the other
two "Great Powers" of the Nile Lake Region—the
kings of Unyoro and Karagwe. He has been painted
to us by different hands as a bloodthirsty monster,
and as a highly intelligent and amiable prince; as a
thorough savage, and as the accomplished ruler of a
semi-civilized people. We will have an opportunity
presently of studying this enigmatical monarch more
at our leisure. Speke and Grant, at least, formed the
worst possible opinion of him, and with good reason.
His "capital"—which is simply the spot where the
king chooses to take up his residence—was a Doubting
Castle to them, and Mtesa a good representative of
Giant Despair. At length they took their departure,

and striking a river that flowed to the north, they
followed it up-stream until they reached a spot where
the lake was seen emptying its surplus waters over a
rocky ledge into the channel that led them towards
Egypt. Satisfied then that the object of their journey
was achieved, they turned their back on the Victoria
Nyanza, and shaped the nearest course for Gondokoro,
where we witnessed them arrive in tatters, but in
triumph.

Their journey, however, was far from setting at rest
the controversy as to the origin of the Nile. Such is
the opinionativeness of the geographer's nature, that
most of the disputants stuck to their old positions.
The adherents to Speke's views, of course, swore by
him and his lake more strongly than ever. Others ridi-
culed the bare idea of a vast body of fresh water two
hundred and fifty miles long by as many in breadth,
such as Speke had sketched on his map from native
information, existing at this particular spot, and nearly
as high above sea-level as the summit of Ben Nevis.
It was directly in the teeth of the evidence of ancient
manuscripts and preadopted opinions, and native information could be got to support any conceivable
proposition. Sir Samuel Baker, for instance, received
the most positive assurance in 1869 that the native
boats sailed from the Albert Nyanza to Ujiji on
Lake Tanganyika; and Livingstone held firmly to
the opinion of the identity of these two lakes, until
he had himself the honour of disproving it by visiting the north end of Tanganyika. To the last days
of his life he believed that the Victoria Nyanza, as a

single body of water, existed only on Speke's map, and that its area was actually occupied by at least five different lakes, some of which had probably no connection with the Nile at all.

The solution of the Nile puzzle was still, in short, in a tantalizing and unsatisfactory stage of semi-solution. An explanation had been offered but the proof of its soundness was not yet complete. Mr. Henry M. Stanley resolved to set the whole question at rest, or perish in the attempt. He would establish the claims of the Victoria to the respectful regard to which its vastness and the importance of its functions entitled it, or show it up as a geographical humbug. Mr. Stanley is no ordinary figure, even among African explorers. His achievements in this field will vie with those of his most distinguished compeers. In tenacity of purpose, in courage, and in endurance he is scarcely second to Livingstone himself. Mr. Stanley introduced a novel method of African exploration, and brought a new power at his back. He was the representative, not of geographical research or of missionary zeal, but of newspaper enterprise. Already he had made a successful journey into Central Africa as the representative of the *New York Herald*, and, in his own peculiar language, had "discovered Livingstone;" that is, discovered whereabouts Livingstone was pursuing his researches. On the present occasion he was accredited by the New York paper and by the *Daily Telegraph* of London, jointly, and the expedition bore at its head the British and American flags. It was also semi-scientific and semi-military in its organization. Here, in the leader's words, is the order of march, as the party started gaily from Bagamoyo, opposite Zanzibar, on the 17th of November 1874:—" Four chiefs, a few hundred yards in front; next, twelve guides, clad in red robes of Jobo, bearing coils of wire; then a long file, two hundred and seventy strong, bearing cloth, wire, beads, and sections of the *Lady Alice*; after them, thirty-six women and ten boys, children of the chiefs, and boat-bearers, followed by riding-asses, Europeans, and gun-bearers; the long line closed by sixteen chiefs, who act as rearguard: in all, three hundred and fifty-six souls connected with the Anglo-American expedition. The lengthy line occupies nearly half a mile of the path."

Mr. Stanley did not mean to be stopped on the route he had chosen by the objections of any native chief to the passage of the little army through his territory. If the opposition were carried to the extent of a challenge of battle, the American explorer was prepared to accept it and fight his way through. In this way he counted on avoiding the long delays, the roundabout routes, and the fragmentary results which had marked the efforts of previous travellers. It is an admirable method, if your main object is to get through the work rapidly, if you are strong enough to despise all assaults, and if you have no prospect of travelling the same road again. Its wisdom and justifiableness need not be discussed; but it may simply be remarked that this conjunction of campaigning and exploration gives an extra spice of danger and an exciting variety to the narrative,

which carries us back to the time when the Con-
quistadors were busy carving out with their swords
rich provinces for Spain and Portugal in the New
World.

Mr. Stanley carried with him, it will be seen, the
sections of a boat, forty feet in length, wherewith to
explore the Victoria Nyanza, or any other great lake
or stream that he might meet with on his course.
He had with him as assistants three Englishmen—
Francis and Edward Pocock, young Thames water-
men, and a clerk named Frederick Barker—none of
whom, alas! ever emerged from the deadly jungles of
Central Africa which they entered so light-heartedly.

Unyanyembe is the usual half-way house of travellers to the lakes; but, breaking off to the right
before reaching that unhealthy den of black-mailers,
Mr. Stanley marched his array north-westwards till
about the fifth degree of south latitude he reached
the water-parting, where the streams begin to flow
northwards.   Here, in a plain over five thousand
feet above the sea, and two thousand five hundred miles in a straight line from its mouth in
the Mediterranean, is the most southerly limit of the
basin of the Nile.   Here, also, Stanley's difficulties
began to gather thick and fast upon him.   The party
suffered for want of food, and lost their way.   The
camp was attacked with sickness, and Edward Pocock
was one of the victims.   The natives were hostile,
and there were fears that Mirambo, chief of the
" Ruga-Rugas," a noted freebooter of these parts,
was hovering with his band of cut-throats in the

neighbourhood. By-and-by these storm-clouds burst
in war, not with the bandits, but with the people of
Ituru. A "three days' battle" resulted in the complete discomfiture of the savage foe; and the weak-
ened expedition marched on, having lost in the
affair "twenty-four killed and four wounded," besides
having twenty-five on the sick-list. For many days'
march the valley of the Shimeeyu, the principal
affluent of the lake from the south, was followed
through dense forests, over which loomed "enormous
bare rocks, like castles, and hillocks composed of
great fragments of splintered granite and broad
heaving lumps of gneiss; then through fine rolling
plains, with a broad prospect on either hand of rich
pasture lands, hedge-inclosed villages, and herds of
wild and tame animals, only interrupted by the
gray masses of crag that started up here and there
from the surface of the green downs."

The lake was near at hand. "We dipped," says
Mr. Stanley, "into the basins and troughs of the
land, surmounted ridge after ridge, crossed water-
courses and ravines, passed by cultivated fields and
through villages smelling strongly of cattle, by good-
natured groups of natives, until, ascending a long
gradual slope, we heard, on a sudden, hurrahing in
front, and then we too, with the lagging rear, knew
that the great lake was in sight." Six hundred feet
beneath them, and three miles away, lay "a long, broad
arm of water," shining like silver in the bright sunshine, bordered by lines of green waving rushes, thin
groves of trees, and native huts; beyond these a dark

boundary of hills, and in front a gleaming plain of
water, with gray rocky islets scattered over it. The
Victoria Nyanza had been struck at Kagehyi, not far
from the spot where Speke first saw its waters. No
time was lost in putting the *Lady Alice* together;
and, leaving the bulk of his followers in charge of
Frank Pocock and Barker, Stanley, with a crew of
ten sailors and a steersman, set out on the 8th of
March 1875 on his perilous voyage round the coasts
of the great fresh-water sea.

It would be too long a story to trace the progress
of the bold "special correspondent" from point to
point of his adventurous course, or even simply to
recount the names of the new countries, rivers, bights,
capes, and islands that passed under his eyes as he
coasted along the lake shores. He has described his
experiences with remarkable spirit and graphic power;
and if one is inclined now and then to smile at the
gorgeousness of his tastes in language, and the imposing titles that he bestows on shock-headed savages
and the members of their "courts," no one can deny
the thrilling interest of his narrative. It is like
making a voyage with Robinson Crusoe in unknown
tropical seas, or accompanying a knight-errant on
one of his marvellous journeys into the untrodden forest in quest of adventure; and yet all the
time you are aware that you are witnessing events
that happened in sober fact only the other day, and
that were recorded in the newspapers as they occurred, like a debate in Parliament or the details of
a railway accident.

Each day some new danger had to be faced, from
storms, or shoals, or hostile natives. For weeks the
shores of the Nyanza stretched on, promontory behind promontory, and still the tired mariners toiled
along the margin of the unknown lands on their lee,
and out and in among the numerous islands. From
the starting point round the eastern shore the coast
shows a succession of bold headland and deep bay, at
the head of which is generally a river draining the
highlands behind. Sometimes a dark mountain mass,
covered with wood, overhangs the waters, rising abruptly to a height of three thousand feet or more ; and
then again there will intervene between the hills and
the lake an open plain, grazed over by herds of zebras,
antelopes, and giraffes. There is great diversity also
in the islands. Many of them are bare masses of
rock, supporting no green blade ; others are swathed
to the summit in masses of rank intertwisted vegetation that excludes the perpendicular rays of the
sun. Some of the smallest are highly cultivated, and
occupied by a dense population ; one or two of the
largest, such as Ugingo, betray no sign of human
beings inhabiting their dismal shades.

Generally the region is rocky, broken, hilly, and
intensely tropical in character. Behind the coast
ranges absolutely nothing is known beyond a few
vague reports picked up from native sources. The
rivers are not large, and it is not probable that they
have their sources so far off as the great snowy range
that runs down midway between the lake and the east
coast of Africa. Some geographers have chosen to call

this chain by the venerable name of the " Mountains
of the Moon," thus removing these ancient landmarks
from their immemorial position in the centre of
Africa, and placing them at right angles to their
former direction.   They ought, therefore, to have
some connection with the Nile; but the likelihood
is that the drainage of the western slopes of Kilimandjaro, Kenia, and the other great mountain masses
that lift their heads above the line of perpetual snow
on the very equator, finds its way into a number of
detached lakes existing in this part of the African
plateau.   The intervening country is roamed over by
the Madai, a fierce pastoral tribe, who make their
living by plundering their more industrious neighbours.   It may be long, therefore, ere any one ven-
tures into the domains of these Bedouins of the
Equator to explore their secrets.   Stanley heard of
" hills that smoked" in this quarter, and it is likely
enough that active volcanoes may be found here,
many of the summits of the snowy range being extinct craters.   Farther to the northward, it is con-
jectured, is the present location of a mysterious lake
—Baringo—which, since the very earliest days of
map-making, has played an active part on the chart
of Africa, appearing, disappearing, and reappearing
again in quite a different part of the continent in a
most unaccountable way.   If any discoverer is ever
lucky enough to catch it, it may possibly be found
to be the source of the Asua river, and an important
Nile lake.   When Stanley reached the extreme north-
eastern corner of the Victoria Nyanza, where Speke

was positive that the Baringo would be got, he found that it had again shifted its ground.

Before reaching this point, the crew of the *Lady Alice* had encountered other perils than those arising from reefs and storms. Unexpected opposition, for instance, was offered by the Victorian hippopotamus. This behemoth of an animal abounds here, as it does in all the waters of tropical Africa; but while in most other places it refrains from attacking man, unless when provoked, it was found on the Victoria lake to be of a peculiarly bellicose disposition. A few hours after starting on his voyage, Stanley was driven off the land and put to ignominious flight by a herd of savage hippopotami sallying out towards him open-mouthed. On another occasion, the rowers had to pull for bare life to escape the furious charge of a monster whose temper had been ruffled by the boat coming in contact with his back as he was rising to the surface to breathe. Probably the hippopotamus of the Victoria would be no more courageous than his neighbours if he were met with on land. There he always cuts a ridiculous figure, as he waddles along with his short legs and bulky body in search of the grass on which he feeds. He seems to know that he is at a disadvantage on *terra firma*, which, if he can help it, he never visits except by night. When interrupted, he makes the best of his way back to the water, where his great strength always makes him a formidable antagonist. On the Victoria Nyanza the inhabitants do not seem to have discovered the methods of killing him practised by the natives on the Zambesi, by capturing him in pitfalls, or setting traps that bring down a heavy log of wood armed with an iron stake upon his stupid skull; and round a great part of the shores he is the real monarch of the lake, his sway being only disputed by the crocodile.

But the hippopotami and alligators are not the only "ugly customers" to be met with by the waters of the Victoria Nyanza. Frequently, when the crew of the *Lady Alice* approached the shore, lithe naked figures would be seen flitting between the trunks of the trees, and savage eyes peering at them through the dense masses of foliage. If an attempt were made to land, a wild-looking crowd would troop out upon the shore; spears would be poised threateningly and arrows placed ready in the bow-string. Though the savage of the lake has not been endowed with the elf-locks that add so greatly to the formidable appearance of the Red Indian, or with the huge frizzly mop of hair that helps to strike terror into the hearts of the enemies of the wild men of Papua, he has succeeded tolerably well, by the aid of tattooing and painting in clay, in increasing his natural hideousness. The character of these negroes agrees very well with their outsides. They are cruel, treacherous, and vindictive, and any one cast away on their shores would have an extremely small chance of being able to tell the story of his entertainment among them.

At one point, near the north-eastern extremity of the lake, Mr. Stanley was induced to approach close

to the land by the friendly gestures of half-a-dozen
natives. As the boat was pulled nearer, the group
on the shore rapidly increased, and it was thought
prudent to halt. Instantly there started out of the
jungle a forest of spears, and a crowd of yelling
savages rushed down in hot haste to the margin, lest
their hospitable intentions towards the strangers
should be balked. The boat, however, to the astonishment of these primitive black men, hoisted a
great sail to the favouring land breeze, which carried
it out to an island where the crew could camp and
sleep in safety for the night. A little further on,
while off the island of Ugamba, a large native canoe,
manned by forty rowers and adorned with a waving
mane of long grasses, was pulled confidently towards
the mysterious craft. After reconnoitring it for a
little, they edged up alongside, half of the occupants
of the canoe standing up and brandishing their tufted
spears. These visitors had been drinking freely of
pombe to keep up their courage. They were noisy,
impudent, and obstreperous; and finding that the
white man and his companions remained quiet and
patient, they began to reel tipsily about the boat,
shout out their drunken choruses, and freely handle
the property and persons of the strangers. Gradually
they grew still more unpleasantly aggressive. One
drunken rascal whirled his sling over Stanley's head,
and, cheered by his companions, seemed about to aim
the stone at the white man. Suddenly Stanley, who
had his revolver ready in his hand, fired a shot into
the water. In an instant the boat was clear of the

intruders, every one of whom had plunged into the
water at the first sound of the report, and was
swimming lustily for the shore. With some little
trouble their fears were pacified, and the humbled
roisterers, partly sobered by their dip, came meekly
back for their abandoned canoe. Presents were exchanged, and the two parties separated, expressing
profound admiration for each other.

A still more dangerous people are the Wavuma, a
pirate race, from whose clutches Stanley had great
difficulty in escaping. They sent out from the shore a
boat's crew on scouting duty, who approached holding
up vegetables as a bait to the hungry voyagers. Meanwhile a fleet of large canoes put out, and tried to
intercept and surround the *Lady Alice*. As the crew
of the latter bent to their oars in order to get out of
harm's way, lances began to hurtle through the air,
and a member of the scouting party held gleefully
aloft a bunch of beads which he had dexterously
abstracted from the white man's boat. Taking aim
at this interesting gentleman, and at another who
was making himself prominent in the pursuit, Mr.
Stanley fired right and left, doubling them up in the
bottom of their respective boats. Aiming his big
rifle next at the advancing canoes, he drove great
holes in them below the water-line, causing their
crews to devote their whole attention to their craft
to prevent them from sinking, while the exploring
boat sailed on unmolested.

The most perilous and the most dubious of Mr.
Stanley's adventures, however, occurred at the island

of Bumbireh, on the western side of the lake. The
voyagers by this time were nearly at the end of their
resources. They had passed weary days of toil under
the blistering tropical sun, and dismal nights of
hunger and cold on shelterless, uninhabited islands,
when the grassy slopes of Bumbireh hove in sight.
Numerous villages were seen in the shelter of the
forest, with herds of cattle, maize fields, and groves
of fruit trees, and altogether the island seemed to
offer a haven of rest and plenty to the weary mariners.
There was besides no food left in the boat, and a
landing had to be attempted at all risks. The look
of the Bumbireh natives was not so prepossessing as
that of their land. They rushed down from their
villages, shouting war-songs and brandishing their
clubs and spears. No sooner had the boat reached
shallow water, than they seized upon her, and dragged
her, crew and all, high up on the rocky beach. "The
scene that ensued," says the traveller, "baffles description. Pandemonium—all the devils armed—raged
around us. A forest of spears was levelled; thirty
or forty bows were drawn taut; as many barbed
arrows seemed already on the wing; knotty clubs
waved above our heads; two hundred screaming
black demons jostled each other, and struggled for
room to vent their fury, or for an opportunity to
deliver one crushing blow or thrust at us."

In point of fact, no thrust was delivered, and possibly
none was intended; but the situation was certainly
an unpleasant one. The troop of gesticulating, yelling savages increased every second; and the diabolical

noise of a number of drums increased the hubbub.
The islanders began to jostle their guests, to pilfer,
and at last to seize upon the oars. Stanley whispered
some words of direction to his companions, and fired
his double-barrelled elephant rifle into the crowd.
Two men fell; and while the others gave way, assisted
by the discharge amongst them of two rounds of
duck shot, the *Lady Alice* was pushed down the
beach, and the expedition was again afloat on the
lake.   But their position seemed little improved.
On shore was the infuriated enemy, hurling after
them stones and spears; canoes were being launched
in pursuit; while the crew of the *Lady Alice* had to
tear up her bottom boards to serve as paddles; and,
to crown their misfortunes, two huge hippopotami
were bearing down on them with jaws agape.   A
couple of balls settled these new foes; but the two-
legged antagonists were not so easily shaken off.   In
spite of the brisk fire directed upon them, four canoes
were got into the water and manned.   The elephant
gun, loaded with explosive balls, was again, however,
equal to the occasion.   "Four shots killed five men
and sank two of the canoes."   The other crews had
to stop to pick up their friends from the water, and
could only shout in baffled rage, as the strangers
paddled away from them, "Go and die in the
Nyanza!"   Dismal days of famine and hardship
followed.   A storm overtook the fugitives, and they
were tossed for hours on the waves of the Nyanza,
and drenched with spray and rain.   On board there
were only four bananas as food for twelve hungry

souls. At length they reached an island, on which, as it was uninhabited, they obtained not only food but peaceful shelter; and, refreshed, they next morning pursued their course, which landed them, not a man missing, at Kagehyi, whence they had set out sixty days before.

Most people in Mr. Stanley's place would have thought that they had had enough of Bumbireh, and that the most prudent course was to give it in future a wide berth. Not so our traveller. He considered that a duty lay upon him of punishing the people who had treated him so scurvily—though it must be said that the natives had considerably the worst of the encounter. Assembling his forces, and reinforced by a number of Mtesa's men, he carried the war briskly into the enemy's ground. A fighting party of two hundred and thirty spearmen and fifty musketeers set out for the offending island. They were opposed by two or three thousand natives ranged along the shore. For an hour the savages gallantly held the water-line, opposing with slings and arrows the volleys from the boats; but at length they were put to flight, and Mr. Stanley, sheathing his sword, went on to other and more peaceful conquests.

During his two months' absence circumnavigating the lake, the second of his white companions, Frederick Barker, had died at Kagehyi. That sad event was one of the items of the heavy cost at which a really great feat of exploration had been performed. The importance of Speke's discoveries and the correctness of his views were completely established. The Victoria

Nyanza was shown to be one vast body of water, and the head basin of the Nile stream. Its extent was shown to be about twenty-one thousand square miles, an area equal to that of Bavaria or Scotland. Excellent havens, navigable streams, and fertile islands were revealed for the first time to our knowledge. Rich and beautiful countries and interesting races were vividly pictured for us. The most remarkable personage, however, in Central Africa is King Mtesa, and the most interesting people are his subjects the Waganda, whose acquaintance we failed to make on our voyage round the lake.

CHAPTER IV.

UGANDA AND KING MTESA.

" Larger constellations burning, mellow moons and happy skies,
  Breadths of tropic shade and palms in cluster, knots of Paradise;
  There, methinks, would be enjoyment more than in this march of mind,
  In the steamship, in the railway, in the thoughts that move mankind."
                                                        Locksley Hall.

T will be remembered that, while coasting along the north shore of the Victoria Nyanza, Mr. Stanley had much ado to escape the attentions which the islanders of Uvuma, situated close to the outlet of the Nile from the lake, wished to force upon him. On the following morning he came upon a land and a people that almost made him fancy that he had dropped during the night upon another planet, or at least sailed in some mysterious way from pagan Central Africa to semi-civilized and Mohammedan Asia. Instead of the stones and spear-thrusts which the Wavuma desired to bestow upon him, he received nothing save courtesy and hospitality. In place of the naked, howling savages whom he had parted from a few hours before, he saw a bronze - coloured people,

scrupulously clean and decently, even handsomely
clad, and showing in their agriculture, their house
architecture, their dress, but most of all in their
polite demeanour, that they had made considerable
progress in arts and industry, and were under the
strict dominion of recognized law.

The head-man of the village approached. He was
attired in a skirt of pure white, covered by a cloak
of finely prepared bark cloth, having over it a fur of
dressed monkey-skin. On his head was a handsome
cap, and on his feet sandals. His followers were
clothed in the same style, though in less rich materials.
He smilingly bade the strangers welcome to the
country, slew for them a fatted kid, and spread
before them a feast of ripe bananas, clotted milk,
sweet potatoes, and eggs, with civil apologies for
having been taken unprepared for such guests. The
traveller looked about him. It was a land of sunshine and plenty—a green and flowery Paradise set
between the brilliant sky and the scarcely less pure
azure of the lake. Care and want seemed never to
have intruded their presence here. There was food
enough and to spare growing wild in the woods, or
in the cultivated patches round the snug homesteads.
Each roomy, dome-shaped hut had its thatched
portico, where the inhabitants chatted or smoked.
Surrounding them were courtyards, with erections
which served as barns, cooking-houses, and lavatories,
all inclosed by a trimly-kept hedge. Outside is the
peasant's garden-plot, where he grows crops of potatoes, yams, pease, kidney-beans, and other veget-

ables of a size that would be the despair of Covent
Garden. Bordering it are patches of coffee, tobacco,
sugar-cane, and castor-oil plant, all for family con-
sumption. Beyond these are his fields of maize and
other grain, and his plantations of banana, plantain,
and fig; and outside of the village is the common
where his flocks of goats and small white hornless
cattle graze, in company with those of his neighbours.

The land is of inexhaustible fertility. The sunshine is unfailing; drought in this moist climate
is unknown; and the air is cooled and purified by
the breezes from the lake and from the mountains.
Within his own inclosure the peasant has enough
and to spare for himself and his household, both of
luxuries and necessaries. His maize fields furnish
him with the staff of life, and the fermented grain
yields the "pombe," which he regards almost as much
a requisite of existence as bread itself. The grinding of flour and the brewing of beer are all performed under his own eye by his family. The fig-
tree yields him the bark out of which his clothes are
made; but the banana is, perhaps, the most indispens-
able of the gifts of nature in these climes. It supplies
him, says Stanley, with " bread, potatoes, dessert,
wine, beer, medicine, house and fence, bed, cloth, cook-
ing-pot, table-cloth, parcel-wrapper, thread, cord, rope,
sponge, bath, shield, sun-hat, and canoe. With it, he
is happy, fat, and thriving; without it, a famished,
discontented, woe-begone wretch." The banana
grows to perfection in Uganda; groves of it embower

every village; and the Waganda,* in addition to
being simply fat and prosperous, have plenty of
leisure time to devote to the arts of war and of peace.
It is to the former, unfortunately, that they are most
naturally prone; but they have also made considerable progress in manufactures, especially in cloth-
making, tanning, metal-working, and canoe and house
building. Even literature is not unknown among
them, as we shall presently see. In short, there is
considerable excuse for Speke's remark when he saw
the beautiful scenery of the Ripon Falls at the outlet
of the Nile from the lake, that with "a wife and
family, a yacht and a gun, a dog and a rod," one
might here be supremely happy, and never wish to
revisit the haunts of civilization.

While we have been making this survey, mes-
sengers have been despatched to the head-quarters
of the king, or kabaka ("emperor") of the country,
announcing the arrival of the white stranger. By-
and-by, with heralding of drums and other music,
and attended by a number of splendidly-equipped
canoes, and with an escort bearing firearms, came an
envoy with an urgent invitation to "court." The
new-comer quite eclipsed the village chief in the
gorgeousness of his apparel. Above features on
which were strongly impressed a sense of the import-

* It may be noted here, in a sentence, as something to be usefully borne in
mind, that throughout Eastern and Central Africa, the prefix "U" signifies the
country; "Wa" (in some quarters "Ba," "Ma," or "Ama"), the people; "Ki,"
the language; "M," a single individual, and "Mono," the prince, of a tribe.
This holds good of all the region, from the Nile lakes to Hottentotland, occupied
by the Bantu division of the African stock, who are markedly distinct from the
true negroes of the West Coast.

ance of his mission waved a huge plume of cock's
feathers, surmounting an elaborately worked head-
dress of beads. A crimson robe was disposed about
him with a dignified grace worthy of an ancient
Roman, while over it was hung a snow-white goat-
skin. The progress to the head-quarters of the court
was conducted with due pomp and circumstance.
Every step Stanley's wonderment and admiration increased; each moment he received new proofs that
he had fallen among a people as different from those
whom his previous wanderings had made him acquainted with as "the British in India are from their
Afridi fellow-subjects, or white Americans from Choc-
taws." Emerging from the margin of dense forests
and banana and plantain groves on the lake shores,
the singular beauty of the land revealed itself to him.
Wherever he turned his eyes there was a brilliant
play of colours, and a boldness and diversity of outline such as he had never before seen. Broad, straight,
and carefully-kept roads led through a rolling, thickly-
peopled country clad in perennial green. Now the
path would dive down into a hollow, where it was
shaded by the graceful fronds of plantains and other
tropical trees, where a stream murmured over the
stones, and the air was filled with the fragrance of
fruit; and then again it would crest a ridge, from
whence a magnificent prospect would be obtained of
the sea-like expanse of the lake, with its wooded capes
and islands, the dim blue lines of the distant hills,
and the fruitful and smiling country lying between,
its soft, undulating outline of forest-covered valley

RUBAGA. KING MTESA'S CAPITAL.

and grassy hill sharply broken by gigantic table-
topped masses of gray rock and by profound ravines.

At length, crowning the summit of one of the
smooth, dome-shaped hills which form one of the
prominent features of the Uganda landscape, appeared
King Mtesa's capital, Rubaga. A number of tall huts
are clustered round one taller than the rest, from
the top of which waves the "imperial standard" of
Uganda. A high cane fence surrounds this residence
of the court, with gates opening on four broad avenues
that stretch, at right angles to each other, to the
bottom of the hill. These also are lined with fences,
and connected by narrow and winding paths, and
the spaces between are occupied with groves of fig,
banana, and other fruit trees, embowering the houses
of the "commonalty." Up one of these wide pro-
menades marched the explorer and his following;
and after due delay—for court etiquette is as tedious
and ceremonious on the Victoria Nyanza as in Europe
—the great gate was drawn aside, and with a crowd
of courtiers, claimants, petitioners, and other waiters
on royal favour, he was ushered from one courtyard
to another, until he stood in the presence of King
Mtesa himself, seated in his great audience hall, and
surrounded by a host of chiefs, warriors, pages, pur-
suivants, standard-bearers, executioners, drummers,
fifers, clowns, dwarfs, wizards, medicine-men, slaves,
and other retainers of court. And here occurred one
of those singular rencounters between white men in
the interior of Africa of which we have already witnessed an example. King Mtesa, for his own glorifi-

cation and delight probably, in the first place, but
also, no doubt, to provide a pleasant surprise for his
guests, had arranged that at Mr. Stanley's second
interview at the "palace," another European traveller,
who some time before had announced his approach,
should be ushered into the hall of state. This was
M. Linant de Bellefonds, the son and the brother
of distinguished explorers in the Nile countries, and
who had been sent by Gordon Pasha on an embassy
to Uganda. For a change we will hear this French
gentleman's account of what he saw, the more especially as he does not see King Mtesa and his court
under such a glamour of romance as Mr. Stanley :—

"On entering the court I am greeted with a frightful uproar. A thousand instruments, each more out-
landish than the other, produce the most discordant
and deafening sounds. Mtesa's body-guard, carrying
guns, present arms on my appearance. The king is
standing at the entrance to his reception hall. I
approach, and bow to him *à la Turque*. He holds out
his hand, which I press. I immediately perceive a
sun-burned European to the left of the king, a traveller, whom I imagine to be Cameron. We exchange
glances without speaking. Mtesa enters the reception
room, and we follow him. It is a narrow room about
sixty feet long by fifteen wide, the ceiling of which,
sloping down at the entrance, is supported by a
double row of pillars which divide the room into two
aisles. The principal and central room is unoccupied,
and leads to the king's throne ; the two aisles are
filled with the great dignitaries and chief officers.

At each pillar stands one of the king's guard, wearing a long red mantle, a white turban ornamented with monkey-skin, white trousers and black blouse with a red band. All are armed with guns. Mtesa takes his place on his throne, which is a wooden seat in the shape of an office arm-chair; his feet rest upon a cushion; the whole placed on a leopard's skin spread over a Smyrna carpet. Before the king is a highly-polished elephant's tusk; at his feet, two boxes containing fetiches; on either side of the throne, a lance (one copper and the other steel), each held by a guard. These are the insignia of Uganda. The dog which Speke mentions has been done away with. Crouching at the feet of the king are the vizier and two scribes. Mtesa is dignified in manner, and does not lack a certain natural air of distinction. His dress is elegant,—a white *conjtan* finished with a red band, stockings, slippers, vest of black cloth embroidered with gold, and a *tarbush* with a silver plate on the top. He wears a sword with an ivory inlaid hilt, and a staff. I exhibited my presents, which Mtesa scarcely pretended to see, his dignity forbidding him to show any curiosity. I address the traveller who sits in front of me, on the left of the king: 'Have I the honour of speaking to Mr. Cameron?'—'No, sir; Mr. Stanley.'—'M. Linant de Bellefonds, member of the Gordon Pasha Expedition.' We bow low to each other, as though we had met in a drawing-room, and our conversation is at an end for the moment."

Having seen King Mtesa at the summit of his

glory, high and lifted up, girt about by hosts of vas-
sals, the absolute slaves of his will, listening delightedly to the sound of a thousand drums and tom-toms,
and gazing from his commanding eminence over his
fair capital and the rich and beautiful region that owns
him as lord, and in company with two white strangers
who have come from the utmost ends of the earth
to pay him court, there will be some curiosity to learn
how the singular fabric of empire on which he sits
has been built up in the heart of savage Africa. All
around is the night of pagan darkness, ignorance, and
cruelty. Here, in the land of the Waganda, if there is,
as yet, no light to speak of, there is a ruddy tinge in
the midst of the blackness that seems to give promise
of approaching dawn. If the people are still bloodthirsty, revengeful, and fond of war and pillage, they
have learned some lessons in observing law and order:
they practise some useful arts ; they observe many of
the decencies of life, and in the cleanliness of their
houses and persons they are examples to some European countries. The Waganda themselves have a high
opinion of their own importance ; and their legends
carry back their origin to what, for an African tribe,
is a remote past. The story, as related by them to
Captain Speke, is as follows :—

" Eight generations ago a sportsman from Unyoro,
by name Uganda, came with a pack of dogs, a woman,
a spear, and a shield, hunting on the left bank of the
Katonga Valley, not far from the lake. He was but
a poor man, though so successful in hunting that
vast numbers flocked to him for flesh, and became so

fond of him as to invite him to be their king, saying, 'Of what use to us is our present king, living so far away?' At first Uganda hesitated, but, on being further pressed, consented, when the people, hearing his name, said, 'Well, for the future, let this country between the Nile and the Katonga be called Uganda; and let your name be Kimera, the first king of Uganda.' The report of these proceedings reached the great king of Unyoro, who, in his magnificence, merely said, 'The poor creature must be starving; allow him to feed where he likes.' Kimera, suddenly risen to eminence, grew proud and headstrong, formed a strong clan around him, punished severely, and soon became magnificent. Nothing short of the grandest palace, a throne to sit on, the largest harem, the smartest officers, the best dressed people, even a menagerie for pleasure, in fact only the best of everything, would content him. Fleets of boats, not canoes, were built for war, and armies formed. In short, the system of government, according to barbarous ideas, was perfect. Highways were cut from one extremity of the country to another, and all rivers bridged. No house could be built without its necessary appendages for cleanliness, and to disobey these laws was death. After the death of Kimera the prosperity of Uganda never decreased, but rather improved."

A different version of the legend was told to Mr. Stanley by Sabadu, the "court historian" of Uganda. According to this personage, Kimera was not the founder of the Waganda nation, but only an important figure in a long list of thirty-five monarchs,

who were enumerated by name, and the first who
taught his countrymen the delights of sport. He
was, in fact, the Nimrod of Uganda genealogy, and a
mighty giant to boot, the mark of whose enormous
foot is still pointed out on a rock near the lake,
where he had slipped while hurling a spear at an
elephant. The first of the Waganda was Kintu, a
blameless priest, who objected to the shedding of
blood—a scruple which does not seem to have been
shared in by any of his descendants—and who came
into this Lake Region when it was absolutely empty
of human inhabitants. From Kintu, Sabadu traced
the descent of his master through a line of glorious
ancestry,—warriors and legislators, who performed
the most astounding deeds of valour and wisdom,—
and completely proved that, whatever may be the
condition of history, fiction, at least, flourishes
at the court of Mtesa. Passing over a hero who
crushed hosts of his enemies by flying up into the
air and dropping great rocks upon their heads, and a
doughty champion who took his stand on a hill and
there for three days withstood the assaults of all
comers, catching the spears thrown at him and flinging them back, until he was surrounded by a wall of
two thousand slain, we come to Suna, the father of
Mtesa, who died only a little before Speke and
Grant's visit to the country. Suna, by all accounts,
was a gloomy monarch, who sat with his eyes brood-
ingly bent on the ground, only raising them to give
the signal to his executioners for the slaughter of
some of his subjects. It is told of this sanguinary

despot that in one day he caused eight hundred of
his people to be killed in his sight, and that he made a
ghastly pyramid with the bodies of twenty thousand
Wasoga prisoners—inhabitants of the opposite shore
of the Victoria Nile, who had rebelled against him.
He had able lieutenants, however, who spread the
terror of his arms far and wide ; and Unyoro and other
neighbouring countries were reduced to vassalage.

He died, and his chiefs rejected his nomination
of his eldest son—a brutal young ruffian, whose
claim to distinction was that he had slain a buffalo
with a club—and chose as his successor the mild-eyed
young Mtesa. The latter immediately gave a proof
of his quality by murdering his nearest relatives and
all his father's most trusted counsellors and warriors.
He was drunk with power, and too often also drunk
with pombe. It was at this period of his career that
Speke and Grant made his acquaintance. In these
days, when the fit of frenzy was upon him, he would
give orders for the slaughter of those who, a few
hours before, were his prime favourites, or, arming
himself with a bundle of spears, the miscreant would
sally into his harem and launch them indiscrimin-
ately among his wives and children. A favourable
change, however, by-and-by came over the spirit
and conduct of Mtesa, and the credit of it is due to
an Arab " mullah," or priest. Muley-bin-Salim, who
visited him on a slave-hunting errand, and converted
him to Mohammedanism. In accordance with the
tenets of his new faith, he gave up drinking and
many of the pagan practices of his fathers, though

still lending some countenance to the "wizards" and
their charms, and did not shed blood recklessly, as of
yore. The Moslem Sabbath was observed, and the
politic courtiers made profession of the creed of Islam;
but it does not seem to have taken any root among
the people. Mtesa himself, indeed, appears to have
adopted it more from whim than anything else. His
is a very inquiring and receptive mind, ready to welcome the latest novelty in ideas or customs from whatever quarter it comes; and Arab religion, literature,
and morality were received with open arms. These,
though far from perfect, were at least an improvement on the old pagan habits and superstitions.

The first ardour of the convert to Mohammedanism
had passed away before the time of Mr. Stanley's
arrival. Mtesa, however, was in high good-humour,
and delighted, as usual, to have a new "sensation" at
his court. The American traveller found him a most
fascinating personage. He describes him as a tall,
slimly-made man, apparently about thirty years of
age, with fine intelligent features, and an expression
in which amiability is blended with dignity. A
remarkable feature of his face are his "large, lustrous,
lambent eyes." His skin, like that of his people generally, is of a rich red brown, wonderfully smooth in
the surface. When in council, his manner is sedate
and composed; but in private he relaxes this regal
dignity, gives free play to the humour of the
hour, and indulges in hearty peals of laughter. Of
the intelligence and capacity of this remarkable
potentate there can be no question; neither can it be

doubted that he has a sincere admiration and liking
for white men. His curiosity about European customs, inventions, and manufactures is insatiable; and
he seems really to have entertained at one time the
notion of modelling his kingdom after a civilized
pattern. His hospitality to "Stamlee" and other
white visitors was prodigal, his professions of friendship overpowering. There is something cat-like in
his caressing and insinuating ways; and, indeed,
Mtesa with all his suave smiles and attentions was
as little to be trusted as the leopard, which the
kings of Uganda take as their badge. He is as cunning and fickle, as cruel and insinuating, as that
lithe and beautiful creature. Carried away by the
first enthusiasm of his admiration, Stanley resolved
on the bold undertaking of converting Mtesa from
the faith of Islam to Christianity, and lost no time
in beginning the task. Daily he gave him lessons on
the truths of the Christian religion and the errors
and absurdities of Mohammedanism. His scholar
was attentive and zealous, and the work of conver-
sion seemed to make great progress. Before Stanley
departed to rejoin his companions at Kagehyi, on that
disastrous voyage in which he fell into the hands of
the natives of Bumbireh, the king had advanced so
far as to observe, along with his great captains, the
Christian as well as the Moslem Sabbath, and had
caused the Ten Commandments to be written down
on a board for his daily perusal.

On the traveller's return to Rubaga, some weeks
later, he found that Mtesa had gone to war with our

old piratical acquaintances the Wavuma. A vast host
had been gathered together both by land and sea.
The king had resolved to crush his enemies by sheer
weight of numbers and terminate the war by one
blow. The American explorer followed in the train
of the Uganda army across the arm of the lake out
of which the Victoria Nile flows, to the rendezvous, a
projecting cape separated from Uvuma by a smaller
island, which the enemy had made his head-quarters.

Stanley had, on the route, an admirable opportunity
of witnessing the power that King Mtesa could bring
into the field. He estimates the army marching
under the Uganda banner at one hundred and fifty
thousand men; and, adding women, children, slaves,
and other camp-followers, that no fewer than a
quarter of a million souls were assembled on Nakar-
anga Point. If these figures are anything near the
truth, there can be no difficulty in accepting the cal-
culation that, including the tributary countries of
Karagwe, Unyoro, and others, Mtesa rules over a
population of three and three-quarter million souls
and a territory embracing seventy thousand square
miles. Besides the land army, the war canoes of
Uganda numbered five hundred; but, as is often the
case in European warfare, only about half of these
were ready for service. To man these great craft—
some of which are over seventy feet in length— about
eight thousand six hundred paddlers were required.
The Wavuma, on their side, had about two hundred
canoes engaged; but, considering their greater apti-
tude and skill in fighting on the water, the odds

against them were not so great as at first sight
appears. Day after day the Uganda war-fleet put
off and attempted to effect a landing on the enemy's
stronghold; but each time they were foiled by the
nimble boats of the Wavuma, which darted like
sharks out of the sheltering coves and creeks, scattered the array of the assailants, and paddled again
out of range before Mtesa's howitzers and musketry,
planted on the cape, could do them much harm. The
king was in despair; and after vainly consulting the
medicine-men, he applied for counsel to Stanley, who
advised that a causeway should be built of rocks and
logs over the half-mile of water between the cape
and the island. This work was begun, but the
labourers soon grew tired of it; besides it was too
slow a process for Mtesa's ardent temperament, and
the plucky enemy were each day becoming more
audacious in their assaults.

Meanwhile the work of converting the king to
Christianity was steadily proceeding. Daily readings
were given from the Scriptures to the king and his
counsellors, and with the aid of Waganda scribes an
abridgment of the Bible was copied in the Kiswa-
hili tongue, the language of the Zanzibar coast, which
is familiar to Mtesa and his chiefs. At length there
came a day when the king assembled his council, and
formally laid before them the proposal to renounce
the creed of Mohammed and adopt the grander faith
taught him by his friend "Stamlee." The replies of
the ministers were diplomatically vague.

Chambarango, the General, said, " Let us take

what is best;" quoth the Prime Minister, "How are
we to know which is true?" and the High Steward
cautiously answered, " I am waiting to hear my master's words."

The matter thus left to his own choice, Mtesa
emphatically declared his preference for the "Book
of the white man," and announced his intention of
firmly adhering to its teachings, and to lay the
foundation of a new Christian Church in Uganda.
Unluckily, a few days later his navy suffered another
reverse, and we find the king storming about in a
frenzy of unbridled passion, giving orders for the
roasting of a prisoner he had taken, and shouting for
the blood of his enemies. Stanley gave his pupil a
well-deserved scolding; and thinking it was time to
interfere in the war, which was hindering him from
continuing his journey, he put into operation a little
project he had conceived, and which is worthy of
being placed beside the famous device of the "horse"
by which the Greeks captured Troy town. Joining
three canoes together, side by side, by poles lashed
across them, he constructed on this platform a kind of
wicker-work fort, which concealed a crew and garri-
son of two hundred men. This strange structure,
covered by streamers, and with the drums and horns
giving forth a horrible din, moved slowly towards
the enemy's stronghold, propelled by the paddles
working between the canoes. The Wavuma watched
with terror the approach of this awful apparition,
which bore down upon them as if moved by some
supernatural force. When it had advanced to within

hailing distance, a voice was heard issuing from the
mysterious visitant, which in oracular tones called on
the Wavuma to make peace and submit to Mtesa, otherwise sudden destruction would fall upon them. The
bold islanders were completely cowed with fear and
amazement. A short council was held, and then a
chief, stepping forward to the shore, cried, " Return,
O spirit ; the war is ended !" The wonted tribute of
ivory and young female slaves for the king's harem
was delivered the same evening, and peace again
reigned on the shores of the Victoria Nyanza.

Next morning Stanley was aroused by the tremendous uproar of the " great King of War-drums "
sounding the break-up of the camp. The king had
apparently played him a scurvy trick. He had
departed early before daybreak, and the camp had
been fired in a hundred places. A strong breeze was
blowing from the lake, and so swiftly were the flames
leaping from one straw hut to another, that the
traveller and his followers had to seize hastily on
their goods and weapons and run for their lives
through a shrieking, struggling mass of some sixty
thousand human beings, all confusedly fleeing out of
the reach of the conflagration. Hundreds, nay, thousands of helpless women and children must, he says,
have been overtaken by the fire, or trampled to death
in the rush of hurrying feet. Mtesa denied that he
had given the order to fire the camp, but it is impossible to absolve him from the suspicion of having
been to blame for this reckless waste of life. The
incident was at least an inauspicious beginning of his

new profession of faith. A closer acquaintance with the Waganda caused Mr. Stanley to modify somewhat his first transports of admiration of their qualities. Ingenious, enterprising, intelligent he found them, above any other African tribe he had met with. Their scrupulous cleanliness, neatness, and modesty cover a multitude of faults; but for the rest, "they are crafty, fraudful, deceiving, lying, thievish knaves, taken as a whole, and seem to be born with an uncontrollable love of gaining wealth by robbery, violence, and murder." Notwithstanding first impressions to the contrary, they are more allied to the Choctaw than to the Anglo-Saxon, and are simply clever savages, whom prosperity and a favourable climate have helped several stages on the long, toilsome road towards civilization. There is no call upon us after all to envy their luxurious lives of ease and plenty under the shade of their bowers of vine, fig, and plantain trees—

"For we hold the gray Barbarian lower than the Christian child."

Nevertheless, Uganda, from its fertility and its situation at the outlet of the great fresh-water sea of the Nyanza, must be regarded as one of the most hopeful fields of future commercial enterprise, and its people as among the most promising subjects for missionary and philanthropic effort in Central Africa.

As for the mighty Mtesa, little has been seen or heard of him since his friend "Stamlee" parted from him. Colonel Chaille Long, late of the Confederate Army, afterwards in the service of Egypt, who had

seen him a few months previously, did not form a
very sanguine opinion of his turning out a respectable and humane monarch.*

Like poor M. Linant de Bellefonds—who, by the
way, was massacred with his whole following by the
Bari tribe on his return journey to Gondokoro—the
colonel was despatched to the Uganda court on a
mission from Gordon Pasha. On this expedition he
discovered, as has already been mentioned, an addi-
tional link in the great chain of Nile lakes. Fighting
his way through Kamrasi's country, Unyoro—a bitter
enemy alike of his nominal suzerain, Mtesa, and of
white men—Long lighted upon a sheet of water in
which the wandering Nile lost itself, at a distance of
some hundred miles from the Victoria Lake. "I
looked in vain," he says, "for the opposite shore.
Stretching away to the eastward a scarcely visible
line seemed to indicate land, certainly twenty miles
away." Advancing, the appearance of land showed
itself also on the opposite or western side; but this,
on being approached, proved to be a vast expanse of
floating water-lilies, whose immense heads, several
feet in diameter, bobbed and floated on the surface
like broad-brimmed hats, while their roots were
fastened to the bottom many fathoms below. It is,
in fact, a lake without any defined shore; for beyond
the lilies are jungles of papyrus and water-cane
growing upon a "floating soil" of matted roots and

* That Mtesa has not lost his interest in his white friends and in the marvels
of civilization, was shown by the appearance in London, in the spring of 1880, of
four Uganda chiefs, as a deputation from the king.

earth, gradually becoming more compact and stable
as the marsh merges into dry land.   Portions of this
spongy mass are constantly "slipping their moorings,"
drifting out into the open water, where they are
caught by the river-current setting through Lake
Ibrahim (as Long named his discovery), and float
gaily down the Nile, a perpetual procession of green,
moving islands.   Colonel Long was warmly received
by King Mtesa, as all other civilized guests have
been.   The humour of the hour with the king of
Uganda was the indulgence of one of the traditional
practices of his ancestors, which cannot be reconciled
with either the Christian or Mohammedan faith.   In
honour of his guest, he caused a score of his subjects
to be decapitated every morning, until the colonel,
while highly appreciating the compliment, delicately
hinted that he would prefer to dispense with it.
Then Mtesa sent him away loaded with presents for
the ruler of Masr (Egypt), among the gifts being a
young daughter of his own.   This scion of the blood-
royal of Uganda, Colonel Long complacently tells us,
was deposited in an "ethnological museum," which,
it appears, the viceroy was forming at Cairo for the
reception of curious specimens of the human family.

A sad fate befell the last white visitors to Uganda.
In response to Mr. Stanley's appeal, a party, consist-
ing of Lieutenant Smith and Messrs. Wilson and
O'Neil, was sent out from England to found a mission
on Lake Victoria Nyanza.   They carried with them
from Zanzibar a little steamer, the *Daisy*, the first
steam-vessel to float on the waters of the lake.   Mr.

Wilson established himself at King Mtesa's court. Lieutenant Smith and Mr. O'Neil, while exploring the lake, were driven by a hurricane to the island of Ukerewe, the chief of which, Lukongeh, had proved himself a good friend to Stanley. No faith, however, can be placed in African princes. On the 7th of December 1877, Lukongeh attacked the missionary camp and massacred the two white men and their black attendants. With this dismal incident the history of the exploration of Lake Victoria has practically closed for the present.

CHAPTER V.

THE ULTIMATE NILE SOURCES.

" In my traveller's history,
Wherein of antres vast and deserts idle,
Rough quarries, rocks, and hills whose heads kiss heaven,
It was my hint to speak....
And of the Cannibals that each other eat,
The Anthropophagi, and men whose heads
Do grow beneath their shoulders."—*Othello*.

IT was early in November 1875 that Stanley bade farewell to his friend and pupil, Mtesa, at Ulagalla, his old capital, where Speke and Grant had first set eyes on this interesting and ambiguous personage. The explorer had an untrodden world surrounding him in all directions from which he could select a line of route. He chose to follow the line of the equator westward, in the hope of falling upon the prolongation southward of Baker's lake, the Albert, the limits of which he proposed to explore. He departed, laden with the " tokens of the esteem of his convert," such as spears, shields, knives, myrrh, and furs; monkey-skins and walking-sticks; beeves, goats, bananas, beer, and wine, and an escort of one hundred warriors. The friends of Mtesa's friend were not forgotten, and at

Stanley's request, a comely damsel and other handsome presents were sent to Lukongeh of Ukerewe,
whose atrocious requital of this attention has just
been recorded. The escort was but an insignificant
fraction of the backing which the king gave to his honoured guest. Further on, near the boundary between
Uganda and Unyoro, a body of two thousand spearmen joined the expedition, whose full strength numbered nearly three thousand souls. Stanley's novel
method of exploration had undergone a new development; and the secrets of Nature were to be wrested
from her by the spear and the bow—by a sudden
and overpowering rush, instead of by patience and
address. The result of the experiment in this quarter does not invite its repetition; for a journey more
tantalizing and indecisive in its results has never
been made by traveller.

The path led through scenes of surpassing beauty
and fertility, and of a character that progressively
changed from soft tropical luxuriance to Alpine
grandeur. Starting from the lake shore, we are told,
the traveller has to struggle for miles through a
tangled undergrowth of bushes, grasses, and creepers,
overtopped by the stately stems of gum, sycamore,
palm, tamarind, and other tall forest trees, whose
meeting foliage gives a cavernous gloom to these
woods even at mid-day. Then he emerges into the
blinding sunlight, and sees stretching before him for
many days' march an undulating country, dotted
with ant-hills, and thinly sprinkled with candelabra-
like tamarisks, thorny acacias. and euphorbias; and

at the top of every new ascent he opens up a wide prospect of "hill, valley, mead, and plain, easy swells and hollows, grassy basins and grassy eminences, the whole suffused with fervid vapour." The scene grows wilder and the way more rough. The wave-like swells of the surface become higher, the depressions between more profound. The primitive rocks break through the soil, and show bare sharp ridges and rounded rib-like masses, tinted gray with mosses and lichens, as if the skeleton of the land were starting through its skin. The slopes of the hills are strewn with splintered fragments of quartz and granite, and the valleys are encumbered with the *débris*. The streams that at first ran in deep troughs, with scarcely any perceptible current in their reed-choked beds, are now ice-cold torrents, brawling over stones and boulders. Great detached mountains, rising to a height of nine thousand or ten thousand feet above sea-level, begin to show themselves on the right hand and on the left. The stifling atmosphere of the forest gives place to cutting breezes and chilly mists. And then the monarch of mountains in this part of Africa, Mount Gordon Bennett, is seen lifting his blunted cone high in air at a distance of some forty miles north of the line of march, and seeming to dominate the whole region.

This vast detached mass is estimated by Mr. Stanley to rise to a height of 14,000 or 15,000 feet above sea-level, and must seem a sublime object even to the eye accustomed to African wonders. Its lower slopes are inhabited by a people known as the Gambaragara,

several specimens of whom Mr. Stanley saw in the
train of King Mtesa and on the march.　He describes
them as of regular features and remarkably light complexion—"approaching that of dark-faced Europeans."
They differed entirely in habits and manners from the
Waganda, and their women were superior in looks to
any that Mr. Stanley had seen in Africa.　It would
be interesting to know more of these singular people
and their rocky stronghold; but the fact that they
have the typical woolly hair of the negro would seem
to show that they are of the same origin as their
more dark-coloured neighbours.　Possibly the high
and temperate region in which they live—in spite of
the fact that the equator almost passes across their
mountain—may have something to do with their
lightness of skin.　Major Serpa Pinto, the Portuguese
explorer, met with specimens of "white Africans" on
his recent journey on the Upper Zambesi, where, as
we know from Livingstone and others, examples of
negro "albinos" are not uncommon freaks of nature.
On the whole we must wait for more evidence before
deciding whether there is an indigenous "white
race" in Central Africa.　The Gambaragara appear
to be a pastoral people, possessing great flocks of
cattle, and living chiefly on milk.　The fastnesses
of their mountain-home, with which they alone are
acquainted, render them safe from the assaults of the
predatory tribes that surround them; and their king
is strong enough to exact tribute from the surrounding lowlands.　Snow often covers the high parts of
the mountain, which seems to be an extinct volcano,

the crater being now occupied by a lake, from the centre of which, it is said, rises a lofty column of rock. The whole country indeed seems to have been subjected to violent volcanic action, large areas being covered with scoriæ, and hot springs and miniature craters of bubbling mud are stated to be of frequent occurrence. Traversing a bare plateau, the dividing ridge is at length reached at a distance of one hundred and seventy miles from the Victoria Nyanza. This last obstacle surmounted, the explorer, to his amazement, found himself on the edge of an awful precipice, fifteen hundred feet in depth, at the bottom of which " slumbered serenely, reflecting the plateau walls on its placid surface, the blue Muta Nzigé."

Having thus reached, apparently, the goal of his journey, Mr. Stanley was not permitted to reap the harvest of discovery for which he had toiled so much. At first all had gone well with the army of exploration. As soon as they had crossed their own frontier into the territory of Kaba Rega—who is no other than our old acquaintance Kamrasi—they found the country deserted. The inhabitants believed that King Mtesa's men were out on one of their accustomed raids. The Waganda warriors themselves seemed to form pretty nearly the same view of the situation. They made great spoil of the abandoned crops, hunted industriously for loot, and were in high spirits. As they left their own frontier further behind them, their courage gradually oozed away. The ominous disappearance of the Wanyoro population puzzled and disquieted them. Most of them also could

not pass over this tract of country without qualms
of conscience or at least of fear. This was especially
the case with the native "general" of the force,
Samboozi, "the Spoiler," who had taken a prominent
share in a great foray made into these parts, by
which the premier of Waganda had first earned his
fame. Enormous spoil had been taken and great
slaughter inflicted; and Samboozi and his brethren
did not feel comfortable in returning in such weak
force to a land on which they had left so ugly a mark.
There were awful memories also of the smoking cones,
fountains of boiling water, fumes of sulphur and
brimstone, and generally diabolical features of the
country in front, which even the recollection of the
fat kine and beautiful captives of Gambaragara could
not efface. Just before the lake was reached, parties
of armed men were seen gathering on the hills.
Prisoners were captured, who declared that an over-
whelming attack was imminent. The bold Waganda
were smitten with terror; the panic spread to Stanley's own followers. He stormed, cajoled, threatened,
entreated by turns, and all without effect. He asked
but for two days' grace, until he could lower the boat
he had brought with him down the rock wall to the
lake. He was told that one day's delay meant
destruction; that he might stay if he chose, but that
only a small proportion even of his own men would
stand by him.

There was nothing for it but ignominious retreat,
and Uganda was reached without molestation. Terrific was the wrath of Mtesa when he heard of the

pusillanimity and desertion of his men. Calling forward one of the young aspirants to royal favour, he
ordered him to "eat up" Samboozi in the approved
fashion of Uganda. In a few days the unlucky
"Spoiler," who in the days of his prosperity had
carried his head unnecessarily high, was a nameless
captive, loaded with chains, on his way to taste of
the royal clemency. Another had taken his titles,
his lands, his flocks, his spoils of war, and his slaves,
and was lord of his two hundred wives. The king
sent an urgent message after Stanley, offering him
his great general Sekebobo, with a hundred thousand
men, to carry him in triumph to the Muta Nzigé, and
stay there till his work was finished. But the
traveller, with bitter thoughts in his heart, and a
materially lower estimate of the Waganda than he
had adopted on his first acquaintance, was already far
away on a new line of discovery. He pondered long
on the offer, but reflecting how little cause he had to
rely on Waganda faith, and the misery which such
an excursion would inflict, he decided to decline it.

Few people will doubt that he resolved wisely. But
the question has been raised, What is this Lake Muta
Nzigé, on whose waters the persevering American
traveller was unable to embark, though he stood on
its brink with three thousand men at his back?
That is still one of the unsolved African mysteries.
Stanley himself unhesitatingly put it down as the
Luta Nzigé, or "Lake of the Locust Leaf," of Speke,
and Albert Nyanza of Baker, the latter discoverer
having on his map represented that lake as stretch-

ing far to the south of the equator, and even believed it to be the northern end of Tanganyika. Unfortunately for that theory, Gordon and Gessi's examination of the Albert proved that it came to an end more than a degree short of the point where Stanley sighted his lake, and that no such feature as his "Beatrice Gulf" was to be found on the eastern shore. The singular thing is that there should be two bodies of water, not only lying along the same line of longitude, with the same remarkable shape and configuration, and apparently on much the same level, but bearing likewise the same local name Luta, Muta, or Mootan Nzigé. All these riddles will be solved shortly, and the conjecture that there is a connection between the two lakes, and that they, with Tanganyika, and probably also Lake Nyassa, mark the line of an extraordinary fracture or crack in the African continent, extending almost due north and south, will probably be found correct. But next time the attempt is made, the aid of a negro host had better not be called in to assist the perplexed geographer.

The route that Stanley, marching in dudgeon from Uganda, pursued through the country behind the wooded western shores of the Victoria Lake, was that which Speke and Grant had traversed in their northward journey fourteen years before. It is well watered, rich in cattle, thickly peopled, and diversified with hill and hollow. Its most remarkable feature is the rivers—if rivers they can be called—by which the perennial rainfall of this region is drained

into the great reservoir of the Nyanza. Speke has
bestowed on them the name of "rush drains." Back
among the hills they are rushing rivulets, that hurry
down the glens they have ploughed in the mountain
side, meeting in the lower country in main lines
of drainage that convey their waters to the lake, to
escape ultimately over the Ripon Falls to the Nile
and Egypt. But these lower courses of the Nyanza
affluents are no longer running streams; they have
worn their way down through the soft clay soil to
the level of the lake, and are simply long, winding
creeks, their surface covered over by a dense growth
of reeds and water-grasses, which frequently hides
all sign of the water below. These rushy lagoons
the traveller finds to be a formidable obstacle in
his course. They cannot be crossed on foot, and the
papyrus and cane are often so strong and thickly set
that it is next to impossible to push a boat from one
bank to the other. The largest of these rivers and
the most important of the tributaries of the Victoria
Nyanza is the stream which Speke called the Kitangule, and which Stanley, out of compliment to the
Princess of Wales, has styled the Alexandra Nile.
It seems as if we were never to see the last of the river
of Egypt. It might reasonably be supposed that
having traced it to its home in the great Victoria
Lake, we should have been ready confidently to solve
that world-old puzzle, which was so long considered
equivalent to a demand for the impossible—" *Caput
quærere Nili.*" But not at all. Apart from the
Baringo and Muta Nzigé mysteries, it has been dis-

OUTLET OF THE VICTORIA NYANZA.

Page 195.

covered that Baker's lake sends off a second effluent
to the north in addition to that which flows past
Gondokoro; that Lake Ibrahim does not pour all its
waters into the Albert Nyanza, but despatches a
branch into the wilderness; while the Victoria Lake
also is said to have a double outlet. What becomes
of these wandering waters, whether they ultimately
find their way back to the parent stream, or go off to
form new lakes of their own or reinforce alien rivers,
no one as yet can exactly say. But here, in the
Alexandra Nile, Mr. Stanley tells us he has discovered
a new ramification of this wonderful river-system,
leading to a new chain of lakes and lake mysteries.
His claim that this is to be regarded as a continua-
tion of the main stream of the Nile derives some
force from the fact, previously observed and com-
mented on by Speke and Grant, that it apparently
contributes almost as much water to the lake as flows
out of it at the northern end, and that this is universally recognized by the natives of the region, who
call this river the " Mother of the Waters of Uganda,"
or of the Victoria Nile. In this view the Victoria
Nyanza would be regarded as merely the temporary
resting-place of the Nile, on its way from parts still
unknown to the Mediterranean, and the course of the
stream, already ascertained to be the second in point
of length in the world, would be indefinitely prolonged. Till this has been better established, however, we must prefer to hold by what seems the more
probable and natural view, that the vast fresh-
water sea discovered by Speke is—as it is well

worthy to be—the true Nile source; and that it is as
bootless to search beyond it for the beginnings of the
river of the Delta as it would be to search the shores
of Lake Superior for the "real original" head-waters
of the St. Lawrence.

The "Alexandra Nile," however, is interesting for
its own sake, and on account of the people that live
on its banks. Where Stanley struck it, above the
point of junction with one of its chief tributaries,
its channel was more than a quarter of a mile wide
Only a hundred yards of this space, however, is occupied by open water. Broad beds of sedge and ooze
stretched out from each shore; but in the centre was
a dull, iron-coloured current, over fifty feet in depth,
and flowing at a rate of three and a half knots an
hour. Throughout its lower course, where seen by
Speke, Grant, and Stanley, the Kitangule preserves
this character of a brown-tinted stream of profound
depth, flowing steadily between wide margins of
rushes, and overhung by grassy terraced banks, on
which native villages and herds of cattle are thickly
scattered. Further up it breaks through a barrier of
rock, and tears down a steep incline in a roaring
cataract. For fully sixty miles beyond these falls,
the river occupies the whole breadth of the valley
from bank to bank—a width varying from four to
fifteen miles. It is no longer a stream, for there is
scarcely any perceptible current: neither is it a continuous lake, except after the heavy rains. It is a
series of reedy lagoons, each with its little core of
open water, and connected with each other by deep,

still canals and creeks, and with green islands
sprinkled over the surface, some of which drift
hither and thither with the winds, or rise and fall
as the rains alter the level of the lake.

Crossing the Alexandra Nile, we ascend the ridges
that skirt the southern side of the valley, to find
ourselves in Karagwe, the country of King Rumanika. Here, if anywhere in Central Africa, the traveller finds a haven of peace, where he can rest for a
few weeks in security under the paternal rule of this
kindly old chief, and recruit himself for the toils and
vexations that lie ahead. This was the experience
of Speke and Grant, who made a stay of many
months under the care of Rumanika; and it was also
the experience of Stanley. They all speak warmly
of his gentle and reasonable disposition, his hospitality, and his friendliness, and seem to have contracted a sincere liking for him and his people. As
has been mentioned, he is a vassal of Mtesa of Uganda;
but the two men are a strong contrast to each other
in every respect, except in their mutual admiration of
Europeans. Instead of Mtesa, restless and excitable,
with his bursts of stormy passion and his wayward-
ness and whim, we are presented, in Rumanika, with
an African specimen of " sweet reasonableness," serene
of temper, soft of voice, and placid in manner. This
" venerable and gentle pagan," as Stanley calls him,
is, at the same time, a very tall man of his inches,
standing six and a half feet in height. In his dress
of state he must present a striking and gorgeous
figure. Heavy anklets of bright copper adorn his

legs, bangles of the same metal glitter on his arms, while from his shoulders depends a flaming robe of crimson flannel. In his hand he carries an enormous walking-stick, seven feet in length; and around him surge a multitude of spearmen, drummers, and fifers, each striving with voice and instrument to outdo the other in sounding the praises of King Ruma-nika and his guests. He may, however, have laid aside these vanities along with paganism, for mis-sionaries have recently gone to reside with the genial old fellow.

Besides busying himself in providing for the creature comforts of his guests, Rumanika was in-defatigable in ministering to their intellectual tastes. He delightedly showed them the contents of the royal "armoury" and "treasure chamber," discoursed with them for the hour on the customs and traditions of his people, and took an intense interest in the filling up of their note-books. His curiosity about the world of Europe and its marvels was insatiable; and he seems to have considered himself bound in honour to requite his visitors for their information by telling them equally wonderful tales of Africa. The kindly old gentleman, indeed, seems to have a vein of humour in him. Thus we find him, after having been told by Speke of the surprising results of steam power, and of how two people could talk to each other though a thousand miles apart, putting the question gravely, but with probably a sly twinkle in his eye, " Whether or not the moon made different faces, to laugh at us mortals on earth ? " Stanley

and he formed themselves into a sort of Mutual
Admiration and Improvement Society, and devoted
themselves for hours to "astonishing one another's
weak minds" with the mysteries of the universe.
The geographical information thus obtained from
Rumanika must clearly be accepted with considerable reserve ; but if it is not all true, it is at least all
new.   The most prominent object to be seen from
the shores of Karagwe is the triple cone of M'fum-
biro, which, at a distance of sixty miles to the north-
west, towers over all the lower ranges to a height,
according to Speke, of ten thousand, and, according
to Stanley, of twelve thousand feet.   This great
mountain, says Rumanika, is in the country of
Ruanda, a powerful state governed by an " empress,"
who will allow no stranger to enter her domains.
From other sources Stanley learned that this remarkable lady was of middle age, tall in stature, of
an almost light Arab complexion, and with very
large brilliant eyes.   Her dominions occupy the
greater part of the country lying between the south
end of the Muta Nzigé and Tanganyika.   It contains
another great lake, two days' canoe journey in length
by one and a half day's in breadth—say forty miles
by thirty—out of which the Alexandra Nile flows.
It is just possible to ascend from this basin, by a
reedy channel, into yet another sheet of water—
Lake Kivu—out of the opposite end of which flows
a stream that becomes the Rusizi, and falls into the
north end of the great Tanganyika; so that if
Rumanika's information should turn out to be cor-

rect, we should have the Portuguese maps of three centuries ago confirmed with extraordinary minuteness. The three great river-systems of Africa, draining into three separate seas, would be proved to be connected by a chain of lakes; and we would have continuous water communication from the Nile to the mouth of the Congo, and from the Congo to the outlet of the Zambesi in the Indian Ocean.

Still more startling were Rumanika's statements regarding the peoples of these unknown lands. Ruanda, he asserts, is populated by "Shaitans" (demons), and he would have had Stanley put down on this part of his map a note similar to that which the old traveller, Sir John Mandeville, wrote over a then unvisited portion of Asia—"This lande is inhabited by Deuills." What Rumanika meant, probably, was that they had treated himself churlishly; and, from Stanley's own experience, they are not an amiable people, for, on his attempting to land on their shores, they snapped and gnashed their teeth like dogs, and made other gestures of intense objection to his presence. Beyond Ruanda, on a lake called Mkinyaga, are a race of cannibals, and also a pigmy people only "two feet high." Possibly some report has reached Karagwe of the existence of the Akka dwarfs in the Nyam-Nyam country west of Lake Albert, and the king had exercised the art of pleasing by reducing the stature of the pigmies as low as he dared. From the observations of Dr. Schweinfurth, and of the explorers on the west coast, these dwarf races appear to occupy a large space of the interior of Africa about the equator;

and by many they are believed to represent the aboriginal people of the continent who have been dispossessed by negro and other immigrants. Rumanika had also to tell of another pigmy people, who had the further remarkable distinction of wearing tails. But the strangest marvel of all was a people " who had long ears descending to their feet; one ear formed a mat to sleep on, the other served to cover the owner from the cold like a dressed hide." Seeing, probably, that his listener looked incredulous, Rumanika added, to clench the truth of his narrative, " They tried to coax one of them to come and see me, but the journey was long, and he died on the way." Everybody must regret this untoward accident; a specimen of the long-eared tribe, if he could have been brought to Europe, would have created a tremendous sensation in scientific circles.

Some of the notes on natural history picked up in Karagwe have also the merit of novelty. The rhinoceros—the black two-horned variety—is a denizen of this country. Mr. Stanley had the fortune to shoot here a white rhinoceros, which, however, like the " white elephant," is only a dirty-gray coloured brute. This animal had evidently just escaped from the claws of some wild beast, a hand-breadth of his thick hide being torn from his rump. But, if we are to believe the natives of the country, it is the rhinoceros's big cousin the elephant who is his most unpleasant neighbour. If they meet in a jungle path, the rhinoceros has to squeeze his ponderous body into the thicket, or prepare for a battle-royal. In

such a quarrel his horn is an ugly weapon, but it is
no match for the tusks and the superior weight of
his rival. The elephant will sometimes treat him
contemptuously—as a schoolmaster would deal with
a naughty boy—and, breaking off a stout twig, say
as thick as a man's thigh, he belabours the unlucky
beast with it until he is glad to save himself by
flight. At other times the elephant will force his
stubborn adversary against a tree and pin him
there with his tusks, or will throw him down and
squeeze the life out of him. These tales are probably
apocryphal: but there are authentic records of con-
tests in the forest between these two huge beasts in
which the bulkier animal has not always come off
victor. The rhinoceros is a headstrong and self-
willed creature, and his vicious-looking head does
not belie his actual character. The fits of ungovern-
able rage in which he is said to indulge, when it is
his habit to root up trees with his horn and run
" amuck " among his acquaintances, may probably be
merely a playful way he has of displaying his vast
strength. But an old bull-rhinoceros is not a pleasant object to encounter unarmed in a forest path;
and if the crusty veteran happen to come across
a surly bachelor elephant whose temper has just
been ruffled by expulsion from the herd, the spectator may look out for a scene worth witnessing
- first of all, taking care to secure a safe place of
retreat. Sir Samuel Baker, who " bagged " many a
rhinoceros in the course of his journeys, has remarked
that the black rhinoceros almost invariably charges

an enemy that he smells but does not see, while he generally retreats if he observes the object before obtaining the wind.

On the southern margin of Karagwe, the limit of the region drained into the Victoria Nyanza is reached at a ridge five thousand six hundred feet above sea-level, beyond which the waters flow towards the Tanganyika. So far as has yet been explored, this height seems to represent the average level of the outer " rim " of the lake basin. Outside of Karagwe. we look in vain for Rumanikas among the petty kings to whom court must be paid. Garrulity and lying are met with in abundance, but no more genial kindness and zealous sympathy. The chiefs are adepts in black-mailing, which they sometimes vary by pilfering or barefaced robbery. At one of these villages, the caravan which Grant was hurrying forward—the chief of the expedition being several marches ahead—was set upon by a gang of rascals, armed with spears, who killed several of his porters, put the rest to flight, broke open and plundered bales and boxes, and, clad in their spoils, danced jeeringly round the white man as he sat on the wreck of his fortunes. In the same neighbourhood Stanley encountered the arch-bandit of these regions, Mirambo, whose name is a word of terror from the Victoria Lake to the Nyassa, and from Tanganyika to Zanzibar. To the explorer's astonishment, he found this notorious personage—

"The mildest-mannered man
That ever cut a throat;"

in short, "a thorough African gentleman," almost
"meek" in his demeanour. He had difficulty in
believing that this "unpresuming, mild-eyed man, of
inoffensive exterior, so calm of gesture, so generous
and open-handed," was the terrible man of blood
who wasted villages, slaughtered his foes by the
thousand, and kept a district of ninety thousand
square miles in continual terror. Incontinently, the
impulsive explorer resolved to swear "blood brother-
hood" with the other wandering warrior, and the
ceremony was gone through with all due solemnity.
The marauding chief presented his new brother with
a quantity of cloth, and the explorer gave him in
return a revolver and a quantity of ammunition;
and then, mutually pleased with each other, they
parted—Mirambo and his merry men to the gay
greenwood, where, doubtless, they had a pressing
engagement to meet some other party of travellers,
and Stanley for Ujiji.

Part Second.—The Congo.

CHAPTER I.

TANGANYIKA.

" *Ber.* 'Tis here!
Hor. 'Tis here!
Mar. 'Tis gone!"— *Hamlet.*

AKE TANGANYIKA had been known to the Arab slave-hunters on the east coast long before a white man had been privileged to gaze on its bright blue waters. These industrious dealers in "black ivory" had good reasons of their own for keeping their knowledge of the interior hid from curious inquirers from Europe; but in spite of this caution, the figure of a great lake, distorted and magnified by the mists of obscurity that shrouded it, had for years been descried, through the medium of popular report at Zanzibar, flitting about in the centre of the conti-nent. But even after science had caught a sub-stantial grasp of the lake, it was found exceedingly difficult to retain a hold of it. There never was a lake,

even in Central Africa, that has shown itself such
an adept at giving its searchers "the slip" as Tanganyika. It has shrunk in where it was confidently
expected to bulge out, and twisted to right or to left
at the points where all who believed that they knew
anything of its habits were confident that it would
run straight. Where it was expected to come to an
end, it would suddenly open up a vista of another
hundred miles of its sprawling length; and only
when its explorers had become persuaded that they
were on the eve of discovering that it stretched beyond
the equator, did it suddenly confound them with the
view of its extremity. Its length, its breadth, its
depth, and its shape have all given rise to knotty
discussions; but the questions most warmly debated
have been—whether it has an outlet; where that
outlet, if it exists, is to be found; and with what
river-system does it connect the lake? And the
curious thing is that though Tanganyika has been
circumnavigated, and every one of its twelve hundred
miles of coast line traced, no one can yet be quite
positive that these questions have been solved.

But the first difficulty of all is to reach the lake.
It is situated six hundred miles as the crow flies
inland from the east coast. The road is haunted
by danger and strewn with obstacles. Of the travellers of our race who have started from Zanzibar
for its shores, only about a half have been fortunate
enough to reach the lake; some have turned back
discouraged by the difficulties of the route; others,
alas! have fallen down and died—martyrs in the cause

EMBARKING AT ZANZIBAR.

Page 117.

of science and humanity. From the first step of his
journey from the east coast, after embarking at the
island of Zanzibar and landing with porters, baggage,
and beasts of burden at Bagamoyo, on the main-
land—indeed long before he takes the first step—
the explorer is beset and well-nigh overwhelmed
with impediments, vexations, and perils of every
kind.   On the low coast country there are malarious fevers to be faced, flooded morasses to be
crossed, a jungle of rank vegetation through which
a path has to be cut.   Beautiful highland countries,
such as Usagara, are passed through as he ascends
the steep sides of the African plateau, and the
grandeur and diversity of their scenery make some
amends for the toilsomeness of the long up-hill climb.
Arrived at the summit of the ascent, instead of a
corresponding declivity on the other side, the traveller finds himself on the margin of a table-land
gently sloping westward.   The moisture, borne in by
the damp winds from the Indian Ocean, is arrested
by the bluff face which the plateau presents to the
sea, and in the lee of this skirting mountain wall
arid tracts have to be crossed—stony, sandy, or
saline wastes, where water is only found at long
intervals, and where the torments of thirst and
hunger have frequently to be endured.   Then nearer
the lake new dangers meet us, from robber tribes,
from hostile gangs of kidnappers, from treacherous
native chiefs.   Throughout the whole way we must
count upon endless anxieties of the mind and constant trials of the temper.   At any moment, the

porters, hired at so much cost and trouble, are liable
to fling down their loads and run away, or escape
into the forest, carrying their burdens with them.
At each halting-place the same scene of noisy
haggling is enacted, and the wayfarer has to pay
dearly for his night's lodging.   The head-man of the
village may be truculent or fawning—he may insinu-
atingly plead for a "present," or brutally demand
his "black-mail"—but greedy and troublesome and
treacherous he is almost certain to be.   And even
when quarters have been secured for the night, and
the traveller stretches his tired limbs in his ham-
mock, he is never sure that ere morning some
"gentleman of the road," like our friend Mirambo,
whom we lately parted with, may not break through
the palisades, with his gang of ruffians, and put all
within to the sword.

But an enemy more dire than Mirambo dogs the
steps of the explorer, or lurks in wait for him at
every turn of the path.   This is disease—fever and
dysentery—into whose power the traveller on African
soil is sure to fall sooner or later, and probably many
times on his journey, and from whose fell grip he
may count himself fortunate if he escape with his
life.   Dr. Dillon, who with Lieutenants Murphy and
Cameron started for Tanganyika in 1873, in search
of Livingstone, gives a description of the party down
with fever at Unyanyembe, which it will be ad-
mitted is "very tragical mirth."

"Now," he says, "for a dismal tale of woe!   On
or about (none of us know the date exactly) August

LANDSCAPE IN USAGARA.

13th, Cameron felt seedy. I never felt better; ditto Murphy. In the evening *we* felt seedy. I determined not to be sick. 'I *will* eat dinner; I'll *not* go to bed.' I did manage some dinner, but shakes enough to bring an ordinary house down came on, and I had to turn in. For the next four or five days our diet was water and milk. Not a soul to look after us. The servants knew not what to do. We got up when we liked, and walked out. We knew that we felt giddy, that our legs would not support us. I used to pay a visit to Cameron, and he used to turn in to me, and complain. One day he said, 'The fellows have regularly blocked me in. I have no room to stir. The worst of it is, one of the legs of the grand piano is always on my head, and people are strumming away all day. It's all drawing-room furniture that they have blocked me in with.' I was under the impression that my bed was on the top of some ammunition panniers; and I told Murphy I was sorry I could not get away sooner to call on him, but I had the king of Uganda stopping with me, and I must be civil to him, as we should shortly be in his country. Murphy pretty well dozed his fever off, but I never slept from beginning to end. We all got well on the same day, about, I suppose, the fifth (of the fever), and laughed heartily at each other's confidences."

Poor Dillon! a few days after these words were written, he shot himself dead while in the delirium of the fever. Murphy decided to turn back to the coast, and Cameron pursued his westward way alone.

As the lake is approached the bare dry plateau gives place again to verdure and running streams. So rank is the vegetation, that in some places the very posts planted to form the village stockades take root, sprout, and completely screen the huts with a dense green wall of foliage. Sometimes huge crags of granite, with splintered tops, show above the greenery, like feudal castles crowned with ruined pinnacles and turrets. In other tracts, the hill slopes are covered solely by a close growth of stunted acacias, " looking," as Captain Burton graphically says, " like umbrellas in a crowd." At length, the great countries of Ugogo and Unyamwezi having been traversed, and the mountain screen that shuts in Tanganyika surmounted, the lake itself comes into sight, with the thatched houses of Ujiji, the rendez-vous of all the expeditions, scientific, missionary, and trading, that have ever visited its shores, scattered along the margin of its dancing blue waters.

The view, by the unanimous testimony of all who have looked upon it, must be one of exceptional grandeur and impressiveness. To the first discover-ers of Tanganyika, Burton and Speke, it seemed the revelation of a new world—a sight to make men hold their breath with a rush of new thoughts, as when Bilbao and his men stood " silent on a peak in Darien," and gazed on the Pacific. " It filled us," says Burton, " with admiration, wonder, and delight. Beyond a short foreground of rugged and precipitous hill-fold, down which the footpath painfully zigzags, a narrow plot of emerald green shelves gently

BURTON AND SPEKE ON TANGANYIKA.

towards a ribbon of glistening yellow sand, here bordered by sedgy rushes, there clear and cleanly cut by the breaking wavelets. Farther in front stretches an expanse of the lightest, softest blue, from thirty to thirty-five miles in breadth, and sprinkled by the east wind with crescents of snowy foam. It is bounded on the other side by tall and broken walls of purple hill, flecked and capped with pearly mist, or standing sharply pencilled against the azure sky. To the south lie high bluff headlands and capes; and as the eye dilates it falls on little outlying islets, speckling a sea horizon. Villages, cultivated lands, the frequent canoes of the fishermen, give a something of life, of variety, of movement to the scenery."

Just fifteen years later, Cameron looked down on the same scene under somewhat less sunny conditions. "At first," he says, "I could hardly realize it. Lying at the bottom of a steep descent was a bright-blue patch about a mile long, then some trees, and beyond them a great gray expanse, having the appearance of sky with floating clouds. 'That the lake?' said I, in disdain, looking at the small blue patch below me. 'Nonsense!' 'It is the lake, master,' persisted my men. And then it began to dawn on me that the vast gray expanse was the Tanganyika, and that which I had supposed to be clouds the distant mountains of Ugoma, whilst the blue patch was only an inlet lighted up by a passing ray of the sun."

Livingstone came upon Tanganyika on the opposite shore. He was footsore, emaciated with toil and

hunger, racked with rheumatic pains caused by constant wettings in the quagmires away to the south
and west.   But even in his depressed frame of mind
and body he was thrilled with the view of the
mysterious sea of fresh water and its grand mountain surroundings.   Resting for a little at Ujiji, he
recrossed the lake, and again plunged into the wilderness, to return again nearly a year later, in a more
broken plight than before—"worried, thwarted,
baffled, when almost in sight of the end towards
which I strained, dragging every step in pain, and
feeling as if dying on my feet."   And then occurred
perhaps the most famous of the historic meetings
that have taken place between travellers in the
remote centre of Africa.   At the hour of the veteran
traveller's greatest need, Stanley arrived on the scene
with aid and news from Europe.   Most people are
familiar with the American explorer's account of his
"finding of Livingstone;" of his polite bow and
question, as he approached the tattered figure, by whose
familiar gold-banded cap, rather than by the gaunt
careworn features, he recognized the great missionary.
"Dr. Livingstone, I presume?" quoth the bold "special."
"Yes," said the doctor, smiling, and returning the
salute; but the firm hand grasp that followed spoke
volumes of suppressed feelings which neither of the
men could trust his tongue to utter.   Once more
Livingstone's powerful constitution rallied, and having
convoyed his new friend half of the distance to the
coast, he turned his back again on Europe and all its
promised rest and rewards,—on family, on happiness,

on civilization,—and betook himself again to the uncompleted task to which he had devoted his life,—

> " Strong in will,
> To strive, to seek, to find, and not to yield."

When Cameron looked down on the Tanganyika
waters from the hills behind Ujiji the iron frame of
the great missionary traveller had sunk down under
its burden. His body, embalmed by his faithful
attendants, had been met some marches before on the
way to the coast, and to Westminster Abbey, where
it found a meet resting-place; and Cameron's chief
mission to Ujiji was to secure the papers of the dead
traveller, which had been left in the hands of native
traders. Stanley, too, felt sad at heart when, descending from the Nile sources, he revisited, after an
interval of five years, the scene of his first triumph.
The soul of the beautiful landscape was gone. "The
lake expands with the same grand beauty; the mountains opposite have the same blue-black colour; the
surf is still as restless, the sun as bright; the sky re-
tains its glorious azure, and the palms all their beauty;
but the grand old hero, whose presence once filled
Ujiji with such absorbing interest for me, was gone!"

With memories clinging round it, however, of five
such giants of African discovery as David Livingstone, Speke and Burton, Stanley and Cameron,
Ujiji must always retain a strong interest for us.
These masterful spirits seized on the lake with a
powerful grip, and in spite of all its slippery wriggling,
did not loosen their hold until it had yielded up its
secrets. Tanganyika, like the Albert Nyanza and

Muta Nzigé—like Nyassa, which we will meet with further on—is an enormous "trough" or crevasse, sunk far below the level of the high table-land which occupies the whole centre of Africa from the Abyssinian mountains on the east to the Cameroons on the west coast, and terminating towards the south only with Table Mountain. Though its shores are not, perhaps, generally so steep as those of the other lakes mentioned, the surrounding mountain walls are as high. Its length is greater than any of them, being little short of five hundred miles. Its waters, like theirs, are very deep, and sweet to the taste, proving almost conclusively that it must have an outlet somewhere; for lakes which have no means of draining away their waters, and sustain themselves by a balance of inflow and evaporation, are salt or brackish. But while the Albert is undoubtedly part of the Nile basin, and the Nyassa drains to the Zambesi, to what great river does Tanganyika present its surplus?

The first notion was that it was a far outlying branch of ancient Nilus. Arm-chair geographers constructed a remarkable lake, in shape like a Highland bagpipe. The swollen "bag" represented a shadow of the Victoria Nyanza, drawn from native report, and it was joined to the long "chanter" of Tanganyika as actually seen by Burton's party. Livingstone was strongly convinced that the outlet of the lake would be found at the extreme northern end, and that its waters went to reinforce the Nile. Seeing, however, is believing; and on the 16th

LIVINGSTONE AND STANLEY ON TANGANYIKA.

November 1871—three weeks after the two explorers
had forgathered so strangely at Ujiji—he set out in
company with Stanley to discover the "connecting
link." The voyage was not without its dangers and
excitements. The dwellers on the lake shores showed
themselves several times to be hostile. At one place
they shouted to the boatmen to land, and rushed along
the shore, slinging stones at the strangers, one of the
missiles actually striking the craft. When night fell,
and the crew disembarked to cook their supper and
to sleep under the lee of a high crag, the natives came
crowding around, telling them with a show of much
friendliness to rest securely, as no one would harm
them. The doctor was too old a bird to be caught
by such chaff. The baggage was stowed on board,
ready for a start, and a strict watch was kept. Well
into the night, dusky forms were noticed dodging
from rock to rock, and creeping up towards the
fires; so, getting quietly on board, the party pulled
out into the lake, and the skulking enemy rushed
out upon the strand, howling furiously at being
balked of their prey.

The first geographical surprise was met with a
little beyond the turning-point of Burton and Speke.
These latter investigators coasted the lake until, as
they thought, they saw its two bounding ranges
meet, and there they drew the extremity of Tanganyika, and returned. This appearance, however,
was found by Livingstone and Stanley to be caused
by a high promontory which juts out from the
western shore overlapping the mountains on the

east. Beyond this narrow strait Tanganyika again
opens up, and stretches on for sixty miles further,
overhung by mountains rising to a height of seven
thousand feet above sea-level, and some four thousand
three hundred feet above the surface of the lake.
At last the actual extremity of the long trough-like
body of water came in view. As the voyagers
approached it, they only became more puzzled as to
what they should find. Two days' sail from their
destination they were positively assured by the
natives that the water flowed out of Tanganyika.
Next day equally emphatic testimony was given
that the Rusizi stream discharged itself into the lake.
Even when the limits of open water were reached in
a broad marshy flat covered by aquatic plants, it
was not easy to answer the question which the
travellers had come all this long way to solve.
Seven broad inlets were seen penetrating the bed of
reeds. In none of them could any current be discovered. Entering the centre channel in a canoe,
however, and pulling on for some distance past
sedgy islands and between walls of papyrus, disturbing with every stroke of the paddles some of
the sleeping crocodiles that throng in hundreds in
this marsh, all doubt as to the course of the Rusizi
was soon removed. A strong current of discoloured
water was met pouring down from the high grounds,
and further examination showed that the stream had
other channels losing themselves in the swamp, or
finding their way into one or other of the inlets at
the head of the lake.

The outlet of Tanganyika must be sought for else-where. Some thought that it must empty itself at its southern extremity into Nyassa, but this theory was destroyed by Livingstone's subsequent land journey across the watershed between the two lakes. Others believed that a "notch" would be discovered either in its eastern or its western mountain barrier, by which its surplus water would be seen flowing off towards the Indian Ocean or towards the Atlantic. Livingstone's own notion was that the lake communicated with the Lualaba by a subterranean passage under the dark cliffs of Ugoma, on the coast opposite to Ujiji; and he even thought he could distinguish the roaring sound of the escaping waters, which the natives told him could be heard for many miles.

This was the uncertain position of the Tanganyika problem when Cameron arrived at Ujiji. He determined, as his first instalment of real discoverer's work, to set this puzzling matter at rest; and his simple plan was to coast along the Tanganyika, and cling doggedly to its shores until he found the outlet, if outlet it had. Hiring a couple of Arab boats, and a crew of thirty-eight men, he set out on his surveying cruise about the middle of March 1874, leading the way in his "flag-ship" the *Betsy*, with the tender following in its wake. A boating excursion on the Tanganyika, especially when there is the elating feeling that every mile of progress is so much territory conquered from the realms of the Unknown and added to the general knowledge of mankind, must have its rare and peculiar delights. The scenery is

by turns fantastic, sublime, but always singularly
striking in its picturesque variety and wonderful
contrasts of vivid colour, and never by any chance
resembling anything we are accustomed to in our
sober-hued northern climes.   On one side lies the
pale-blue expanse of the lake, beautiful but treacherous ; for at any moment a sudden storm may come
scouring down the mountain gullies "in thunder,
lightning, and in rain," whipping the waters into
foam, and arousing a fierce strife and uproar of con-
tending waves, out of which the voyager is glad to
steer his craft into some haven of safety.   But the
characteristic aspect of Tanganyika is when it is
bathed in the dazzling light of the tropical sun, and
when the mirror-like waters reflect every tint and
every detail of the landscape and the sky.

Sailing, as we now are, southward, the view on the
right hand is bounded by the high broken line of the
mountains on the opposite side of the lake, sometimes
far off on the horizon, thirty miles away, and then
again separated from us only by a distance of two or
three leagues. Close at hand on the left rises the other
rocky wall that rims in the Tanganyika, the bright
red cliffs of sandstone gleaming out from the vivid
green masses of foliage that clothe their sides from
the shore to the sky-line, both rock and trees being in
gairish contrast with the shades of the water and of
the heavens.   The shores are constantly advancing
in bold headlands, or receding in bays, at the head
of which a torrent will probably be seen rushing
down a stony channel overhung by fine forest trees ·

or the inlet may end in a white pebbly or sandy beach, or in a creek choked with rank green weeds and undergrowth. At frequent intervals cascades tumble over the cliffs; the table-land above is like a sponge soaked with moisture, and the rocks seem constantly paying their tribute of tears to the lake. On Cameron's voyage, which only extended about half way round the shores of Tanganyika, he counted the mouths of a hundred rivers discharging into it, the first met with and the most important of all being the Malagarazi, whose modest beginnings Stanley saw as he crossed the water-parting from the Victoria Nyanza. Further on the colour of the Tanganyika crags undergo many changes. Instead of red sandstone, precipices of black marble, streaked with white, abut on the shore; in several places the section of a coal formation, which may be of great importance in the future development of the region, is exposed; or the waves break at the feet of cliffs of chalk, cut as cleanly as if done with a knife. The shores and water are alive with animal life. Aquatic birds of many species—gulls, divers, herons, king fishers, eagles, fish-hawks—abound. The serried back of a floating crocodile looks to the cautious mariner like a ridge of rock, half awash; the resounding snort of a hippopotamus warns him to get ready his gun; or the leaping of the large lake fish encourages him with the hope of a change of fare.

Occasionally a chance of still better sport will present itself. At one spot, while running under sail close to the narrow beach, Cameron espied an elephant which had scrambled down through the thicket to enjoy the luxury of a bathe. Instantly the crew were ordered to lie down flat in the boat, to keep silence, and in particular not to disturb one fellow who was snoring peacefully below the gunwale. Unluckily, just as the boat was getting within range, the sleeper awoke, started to his feet, and yelled at the pitch of his voice, "Elephant, master!" and away bolted the great brute unscathed into the jungle, "flapping his big ears, like a rabbit bolting into its burrow." This is not the only kind of annoyance that has to be encountered in a native boat manned by blacks; and many times had Cameron occasion to wish devoutly for "two or three weeks of an English whale-boat and crew."

The men were lazy, and seized every occasion of shirking their work ; and their stupidity, cowardice, and superstition made constant demands on the explorer's temper. Attacks of fever, which rendered him unfit to take bearings, also caused delay. While suffering from one of these seizures, he had the curious idea that he was "double," and that it was for the sole benefit of his second self, lying shaking and groaning on the opposite side of the boat, that a pot of cold tea had been laid down. "When in my tossing about I rolled over to that side, I seized the tea-pot, drank like a whale, and chuckled at the idea of the other thirsty mortal having been done out of some of his tipple." Still more detention was caused by another species of ghostly beings—"demons"—with which Tanganyika is more than averagely well sup-

plied. Almost every cape, island, or high crag in the
southern portion of Tanganyika is in native estima-
tion the chosen abode of some "devil;" and no one
will dare to pass the haunts of these malicious spirits,
save under certain conditions, and after offering
beads or some other gift to propitiate their good will.
The "devil," or, as is quite as often the case, the
"deviless," is highly susceptible to flattery; and
while passing its retreat, the boatmen sing such
praises as, "You big devil! you big king! you kill
all men; let us go by." The most powerful of all
the spirits of the lake has his seat on a singular
tabular mount, shaped like a vast tower, and rising
to a height of twelve hundred feet, and flanked on
either side by two similar rocks, the abodes of the
demon's wife and son.

These devils' dwellings are situated at the extreme
southern end of Tanganyika, where the lake has,
appropriately, a "cloven hoof" shape—a long promontory, as in the case of Lake Nyassa, piercing the
extremity. There is no thoroughfare this way for
the waters of Tanganyika. The haunts of evil spirits
are not needed to make it a wild, eerie, and romantic
place. The walls of the plateau into which the bays
and inlets of the lake are dovetailed show some of
the most extraordinary examples of rock and tree
scenery to be seen in the world. Ponderous masses
of granite, rising as high as eighty feet above the
surface of the water, are scattered at the foot of the
cliffs. At some places there are the appearances of
terraces and fortress-walls, crowned with parapets

and towers, built up in courses, as by the hand of
man.   " Enormous masses of rock," says Cameron,
" are scattered and piled in the most fantastic manner
—vast overhanging blocks, rocking-stones, obelisks,
pyramids, and every form imaginable.   The whole is
overgrown with trees jutting out from every crevice
or spot where soil has lodged, and from them hang
creepers fifty or sixty feet long, while through this
fringe there are occasional glimpses of hollows or
caves."

The whole scene seemed a design for some transformation scene in a pantomime, rather than a sub-
stantial part of Mother Earth ; and the spectator
almost expected to see the rocks open and the sprites
appear.   He had not long to wait.   " As I paused to
gaze at the wondrous sight—all being still, without
a sound of life—suddenly the long creepers began to
move, as some brown object, quickly followed by
another and another, was seen.   It was a party of
monkeys swinging themselves along, and outdoing
Leotard on the flying trapeze ; and then stopping, and
hanging by one paw, they chattered and gibbered
at the strange sight of a boat.   A shout, and they
were gone more rapidly than they came, whilst
the rolling echo almost equalled thunder in its intensity.   In places the slightest shock of earthquake
would cause masses of thousands of tons to topple
down from their lofty sites, and carry ruin and destruction before them."   The slightest noise disturbing the accustomed silence of these spectral crags and
caves is duplicated and prolonged with startling effect.

If one raise the voice above a whisper, it is enough to make

"The great echo flap,
And buffet round the hills from bluff to bluff."

The people of the Tanganyika shores do not produce so imposing an effect as their country, though they do their best to call in art to aid the defects of nature. Take, for instance, a picture of a head-man dressed in the height of fashion as a specimen of many we have met, and are likely yet to meet, on our journeying:—"The chief was profusely greased, had a patch of lamp-black on his chest and forehead, and wore a tiara of leopards' claws, with the roots dyed red, and behind it a tuft of coarse, whitish hair; a pair of leopard-skin aprons, a few circles of yellow grass below his knees, a ring on each ankle, and a fly-flapper with the handle covered with beads, completed his attire, if we except the lamp-black which was rubbed into all his tattoo marks." They are immensely proud of the figure they cut; and Cameron nearly burst a blood-vessel laughing at the care with which one dandified black folded up his only article of clothing, a loin-cloth, placed it on his head, and hoisted an umbrella of which he had become possessed, to save it and his painted skin from the rain. Considering the precipitous nature of the shore, the population is pretty dense on the western bank, and they carry on several branches of native manufacture, such as the weaving of cotton; but the eastern coast of the lake has been harried by the slave-traders and the robber clans. Unmistakable signs of the

ravages of these miscreants during the interval since
Livingstone had visited the lake were observed by
Cameron, and the depopulation was almost complete
when Stanley followed in the latter's footsteps two
years later.

Two months after he had set sail from Ujiji,
Cameron was rewarded for his persevering search
by the discovery of what appeared to him to be undoubtedly the long-sought-for outlet of Tanganyika.
About half-way between the southern and northern
extremities of the lake, the chain of mountains
girdling the western shore came almost suddenly
to a stop. Some miles further on, the shores of the
lake were to be seen again rising abruptly, and in
the centre of the gap was a broad channel stretching far into the land between the opposing heights.
This was the Lukuga, which for days before the
traveller had heard of as the river that carried off the
outflow of the Tanganyika. His impression that this
was the case was confirmed by finding a current
setting out of the lake, and which drifted his boat
into the channel. At first a mile in width, the
Lukuga, at a little distance from the lake, became
choked with grass, reeds, and mud-banks, through
which the water seemed to drain ; and a gap in a low
range of hills, some eight miles ahead, was pointed
out by which, the natives told him, the Lukuga
escaped, and flowed down the opposite slope to the
Lualaba, and thence to the great Western Ocean.

The scientific "bigwigs," when this discovery was
reported to them, gave a great gasp of relief, as if

some knotty fact that threatened to spoil their carefully constructed theories had been satisfactorily got
out of the way. Tanganyika, with its heavy rainfall, its fresh water, and its walled-in sides, was not
then so great an anomaly after all. It had an outlet
—and not a subterranean or otherwise mysterious
outlet, but one quite above-board—though it had made
the eccentric choice of placing it in its side instead of
at either end. Tanganyika, however, had one trick
more to play To it, in 1876, as has already been said,
came Mr. Henry M. Stanley, fresh from his triumphs
on the Victoria Nyanza. He took a mental glance
round the lake, saw that there were obscure corners
here and there which needed to be lighted up, and
thought he might as well accomplish this little task
before setting out on his gigantic undertaking of
tracing the mighty stream of the Lualaba, which
Livingstone had discovered away to the westward,
and believed to be the head-waters of the Nile,
though others, who had information that the lonely
missionary traveller lacked, were convinced that it
could be none other than the Congo. Stanley embarked in his stanch little *Lady Alice*, which had
alternately carried and been carried by the traveller
for so many hundreds of miles already; and he made
a boat voyage of between eight hundred and nine
hundred miles, that occupied him fifty-one days.
Among other places, he visited the Lukuga; but lo!
instead of a current setting out of the lake, he found
one flowing in. The little tributary streams of the
Lukuga also, which Cameron had observed were all

turned from the Tanganyika, twisted their mouths the other way on Stanley's arrival! It is true there were the break in the plateau-wall, the gap in the low ridge beyond, through which water was found running westward, and the grass-covered swamp between. But this swamp, says Stanley, is the parent both of the Lukuga flowing to the lake and of the other Lukuga flowing to the Lualaba. There is only a foot or two of difference in the level, but the marsh has the advantage of it over the lake, and of course water cannot flow up-hill. But though the Tanganyika had yet got no outlet in 1876, it is now probably supplied with one in full working order.* The level of the lake, the American explorer points out— and indeed others had pointed it out before him—is gradually rising, as witness the submerged fields and villages along its banks. A few feet more of rise and it would overtop the impediment in the Lukuga channel, and discharge itself for the first time by this convenient waste-water pipe into the neighbouring basin of the Lualaba. For thousands of years—indeed since the world began—it has slowly been filling up its deep reservoir, good-naturedly delaying the ceremony of "turning on the water" until Mr. Stanley should be on the spot to witness it!

This is a fascinating theory, but perhaps a more obvious one is to be preferred. Tanganyika is too old not to have discovered this chink in its side long ago. In its time it has had several levels, and in

* This has been confirmed by the recent visit of Mr. Hore to the Lukuga creek. He found a strong current setting unequivocally out of the lake, and flowing by this channel down the slope towards the Lualaba.

point of fact it alters its flood-mark at least once every year with the rainy and the dry seasons. The Lukuga gap probably represents the fracture of an earthquake, or a hole which the imprisoned waters had broken out and escaped by in some former age, and which has been its safety-valve in its later history. When the Tanganyika has water to spare, it empties it westward; when it has not, it keeps all its supply to itself, and generally preserves a very fine balance between inflow and evaporation. It is a semi-detached lake—an "Occasional Contributor" to the ponderous volume of the Congo—and as such it has no prototype elsewhere on the globe, at least on the same scale.

CHAPTER II.

THE LUALABA LAKES.

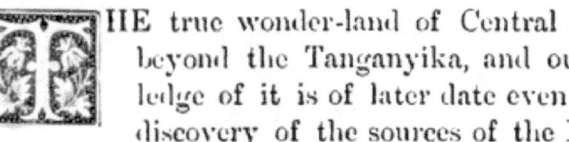HE true wonder-land of Central Africa is beyond the Tanganyika, and our knowledge of it is of later date even than the discovery of the sources of the Nile. In the centre of the great table-land, of which mention has so often been made, is a vast hollow, with sloping sides, measuring a thousand miles in length by probably as many in breadth, into which the rains and the dews of heaven—the deluging rains and heavy dews of the tropics—have fallen for ages. At one period —perhaps when the Sahara was an arm of the great salt ocean—this depression must have formed the bed of a fresh-water sea. Gradually the great reservoir would fill up, till the brimming waters would discover the spot where its retaining wall was lowest, and would spill over into the Atlantic. The channel thus formed would gradually deepen, eating its way through the rocky barrier, until the whole storehouse of water would be drained to the bottom. Behind would be

left soaked plains and dripping hill-slopes of rich
alluvial soil, which the hot sun and plentiful moisture
of this equatorial clime would cover with a prodigal
growth of vegetation as fast as the waters withdrew.

Winding in great folds for two thousand miles at
the lowest level of the depression is a mighty river—
the main trunk on which all the branches of drainage
converge. From its nature it is in its upper course
no scurrying, brawling stream, roaring over rapids,
and making mad leaps down precipices. Its current
is slow and majestic, broad, smooth, deep, and even-
flowing, and capable of bearing navies of merchant-
men on its wide breast. Sometimes it stands still,
and spreads out into great lakes, from whose centre
an ocean horizon surrounds the voyager. Between
these expansions its appearance is more like that of
a lake than a river. Its breadth is rarely less than
one, often as much as six and even ten miles. Islands
miles in length look like insignificant clumps of verdure from its banks, and the inhabitants have rarely
communication with the shore. The Nile may exceed
it in length, but it is no more comparable with it in
bulk and volume than a slender palm-tree is to the
massive baobab, or than the scraggy giraffe is to
the lordly elephant. There are many of its minor
branches that supply more water than all the rivers
of Northern Africa put together. These affluents
have their courses, like the main stream, through
rank forest wildernesses for many hundreds of miles,
receive in their turn tributaries which would be rivers
of the first rank in Europe, expand into large unvisited

lakes, and pass by the dwellings of races who have never seen and probably never heard of the white man.

Europe was, on its side, equally ignorant of this vast forest and lake region and its inhabitants till the year 1873. The mouth of the Congo river had of course been familiarly known for centuries; but the colossal volume of water which it discharges into the sea, and which is exceeded only by that of the Amazon among the rivers of the world, had never been accurately gauged. Little or no curiosity was shown as to where the swift current, ten miles in width and six hundred feet deep, could have been collected. Twenty or thirty years ago geographers hardly deigned to bestow a thought on the problem of the Congo, and dismissed it with the most careless mention. Away in another direction—in the Portuguese settlements on the east coast — rumours had long been current of a powerful potentate, named Cazembe, who ruled over a rich and extensive region in the interior, occasionally visited by native traders. At the close of last century a Portuguese traveller, Dr. Lacerda, succeeded in reaching Cazembe's court; but he died there, and the story of his adventures was for the most part left untold. In 1866, the foremost champion of geographical discovery, David Livingstone, buckled on his armour, and started from the east coast, with the resolution to unveil the long-hidden secrets of this region. Already he had been for the best part of twenty years engaged in explorer's work in South Central Africa, where we shall accom-

pany him on his two famous journeys across the continent, and on his subsequent expeditions to complete
the examination of the river-system of the Zambesi.

On this the most arduous, the most extended, and,
alas! the last of his journeys, Livingstone first set out
on the 7th of April 1866, starting from the mouth of
the Rovuma river, half-way between the Zambesi and
Zanzibar. He held his way round the southern end
of Nyassa, skirted the high land between that lake
and the Loangwa river, a branch of the Zambesi,
and after many months of wandering found himself, at the close of 1866, on the crest of a range
which parted the waters flowing south from those
flowing north into a great valley which he was
told was that of the Chambesi river. Livingstone
had no idea at this time that he had crossed the
threshold of a new region. The Chambesi was not
an unfamiliar name. He believed, as the rest of the
world then believed—misled partly by the similarity
of sound—that it was merely a northern branch of
the Zambesi. What the explorer looked down upon
from his vantage-ground was a vast sea of verdure,
which filled up all the valleys and tossed itself to
the highest peaks of the hills. The soil was moister,
the vegetation more dense, the air more humid even
than in the countries behind him. He had reached,
in fact, the head-waters of the Congo—the Lualaba;
or, as some have proposed to rechristen this river in
honour of the man who may be said to have made its
importance known, the Livingstone.

It was under evil auspices that the missionary

pioneer plunged into the depths of this virgin forest,
which, for the next seven years and a half, was the
scene of his lonely wanderings, and where he at length
laid himself down to die. His followers had deserted
him, carrying back to the coast lying stories of his
having been murdered. Trusted servants decamped
with his medicine-chest, leaving him with no means
of fighting the deadly diseases which from that hour
began to break down his strength. The country
ahead had been wasted and almost emptied of inhabitants by the slave-traders. Hunger and thirst were
the daily companions of his march. Constant expo-
sure to wet brought on rheumatism and ague; painful ulcers broke out in his feet; pneumonia, dysentery, cholera, miasmatic fever attacked him by turns;
but still, so long as his strength was not utterly prostrated, the daily march had to be accomplished.
Still more trying than the fatigue were the vexatious
delays, extending sometimes over many months,
caused by wars, epidemics, or inundation, that frequently compelled him to retrace his steps when apparently on the verge of some great discovery. Often,
in order to make progress, he had no alternative but
to attach his party to some Arab expedition which,
under pretence of ivory-trading, had come out to
plunder, to kidnap, and to murder. The terrible
scenes of misery and slaughter of which he was thus
compelled to be the witness had perhaps a stronger
and more depressing effect on his mind than all the
other trials that fell to his lot. " I am heart-broken
and sick of the sight of human blood," he writes, as

he turns, baffled, weary, and broken down in health, from one most promising line of exploration which he had been striving for a year to follow. "Weary! weary!" is the only entry for one day's march through dismal swamp and shaggy forest. But no sooner had a little strength returned to him than he again turned his back on the road that led to his distant home, where rest and honours were awaiting him, and took up his uncompleted labours in whatever direction he saw a path opened for him into the wilderness. And in all these eight years' wanderings he was only once —at Ujiji, in 1871—cheered by the sight of the face of a civilized man; only at intervals of years did he hear news of home and friends, and of the great events that were happening in Europe. It was a struggle between one heroic soul and the whole forces of savage nature and savage man; and though the great traveller fell in the unequal contest, he fell unconquered and covered with glory.

Of this journey we have only an imperfect and fragmentary record—rough jottings made at the close of the long day's march, the mere skeleton outline of that story of wild adventure and strange discovery, the particulars of which can never now be known. For weeks at a time no entries are to be found in the journal: the hand that should have written them was palsied with fever, the busy brain stunned into uncon- sciousness, and the tortured body was being borne by faithful attendants through novel scenes on which the eager explorer could no longer open his eyes. His letters were lost or stolen on the long way to the coast;

his Arab companions were hostile spies on his movements, and strove with might and main to mislead him and to close all channels of information from him. Yet these loose and disjointed notes—written latterly on scraps of old newspapers, with an ink manufactured by the traveller himself from the seeds of a plant— tell a more affecting tale and convey a more valuable store of knowledge than many a brilliant and carefully-written narrative.

As in all Livingstone's writings, there is a transparent earnestness and truthfulness in these "Last Journals;" and we see not merely the bold pioneer of discovery, but the patient and loving student of nature, and the warm-hearted advocate of downtrodden fellow-men. Glimpses of the savage jungle life and scenery are occasionally revealed to us. From an eminence we look down on the unshorn forest, through which the path has led for many days' journey, stretching illimitably before us, with perhaps no break or clearing save the channel of some slow winding stream. In the valley of the Chambesi, into which we are first introduced, the population has been almost completely swept away by the slavers, whose trade is rather one of "consecutive murder" than of simple man-hunting. The native clearings have been overgrown by jungle and weeds, and the primeval woods again hold undisputed sway. The ancient monarchs of the forest are only, however, scattered at intervals among the trees of baser and more stunted growth. Devastating fires sweep over these virgin lands in the dry season, leaving over great tracts only tall trunks

rising here and there above the ashes of their fellows
A single year restores the grasses, creepers, and bamboos to their wonted rankness, and the country is
again covered with dense scrub and forest. `

An oppressive stillness generally reigns in these
untrodden solitudes. The African forest is far, however, from being destitute of life, colour, and movement; even the sweet songs of birds, which we are
accustomed to think are only heard in temperate
climes, are not absent. The volume of song in many
localities is as strong, though not perhaps so har-
monious, as is heard in our British woods. Notes
are heard resembling those of the lark, the chaffinch,
the robin, the blackbird, and other familiar songsters,
all, however, with a difference, as if our favourites
were carolling in some foreign tongue. Others give
forth a deep metallic sound like a bell, while a
little denizen of the woods repeats a single note
like a stroke on a violin string. The shrill treble
of the tiny tree-frog, perched on some branch like the
feathered members of the choir, mingles not unmusi-
cally with the chorus. Some there are of gorgeous
plumage, but the majority of African songsters, unlike
the birds of South America and other tropical countries, are sober-suited like our own. In dry, hot
weather, when the sun is high, the forest is silent;
but in the mornings and evenings, especially after a
shower, the universal twitter and the piping duets of
affectionate lovers recommence. Perhaps the chir-
ruping note of the honey-guide makes itself prominent, as it strives to attract the attention of the trav-

eller. This singular bird has learned somehow to
make its living by a study of the tastes of its fellow-
creature, man. Following its guidance, one is led
infallibly to the retreat of a swarm of honey-bees;
and in the plunder that ensues it of course expects to
share. Birds of two separate varieties have entered
into a similar league of friendly co-operation with
the rhinoceros and the buffalo. They are allowed to
perch on the backs of these bulky quadrupeds, and
pick up a livelihood on the ticks and other parasites
that infest their skins; and they render a still more
valuable service to their big friends by taking short
flights in the air, and warning them by a shrill note
of the approach of some danger invisible down
among the tall close growth of the jungle grass.

The habits of bees, of ants, of beetles, of spiders,
and of the innumerable insects that infest the forest
localities constantly afford matter for instruction and
amusement, though the traveller would often gladly
dispense with the entertainment in order to rid himself of their attentions. The most ferocious enemy
of the explorer in these countries, in fact, is not any
of the larger species of wild beasts, with their portentous weapons of claw, and horn, and tusk, but a small
fly—the notorious tsetse. Promising expeditions
have been brought to hopeless ruin by these puny
warriors. Its bite is death to cattle and all kinds
of baggage animals; its presence in a country is an
effectual bar to colonization. It is supposed to follow
the tracts of the zebra, occupying well-defined spaces,
which it never crosses; and it is believed that with

the expulsion of game the area of its ravages will be
contracted. At the same time, it is a rather sad
thought that the magnificent herds of wild animals
—zebras, elands, buffaloes, giraffes, gnus, and numerous species of deer and antelope—which once roamed
all over Central and South Africa, down to the Cape
of Good Hope, are every year being thinned away,
or driven northwards. The lion—the boasted king
of animals—makes a poor figure beside the tsetse fly
in travellers' records. The general impression about
him is that, in spite of his formidable strength, his
imposing roaring, and his majestic mane, he is a
coward and a skulker. Livingstone had a hearty
contempt for the brute, though in his time he had
been severely mauled and bitten by him. The lion,
however, when sore pressed by hunger, has been
known to pluck up sufficient courage to tear off the
flimsy roof of a native hut and leap down upon the
sleeping inmates. The elephant—a much grander
animal in every respect—occasionally performs a
similar feat, his motive being curiosity, or perhaps
mischief, if one of his periodical fits of ill-nature is
upon him. A sight may now and again be got of
a roaming rhinoceros tramping stolidly with surly
gruntings through the depths of the thicket; a glade
will be suddenly opened up where a group of shaggy
buffaloes are grazing; or a herd of startled giraffes will
break away in a shambling gallop, their long necks
swinging ungracefully to and fro, as they crash their
way through the forest, like "locomotive obelisks."
Now and then a shot may be got at a troop of zebras,

pallahs, wild-beeste, or other big-game animals, and
the scanty larder be replenished for a time ; but the
traveller must often lay his account with being
absolutely in want of food, and be fain, like Livingstone, to draw in his belt an inch or two in lieu of
dinner.

But the most gallant sport in these regions—
excelling in danger and excitement even elephant-
hunting—is the chase of the hippopotamus. This is
prosecuted by a hereditary race of hunters, who have
attained extraordinary skill in their art. They are
described as a bold, outspoken, hospitable people, who
live a wandering life, moving from river to river in
search of their prey. In frail boats, built solely for
swiftness, they cautiously approach the spot where a
huge hippopotamus is seen slumbering on the bosom
of the stream. Not a sound is heard, not a ripple is
visible, as they drop down on their victim ; and only
when within a few feet of him does the harpooner in
the bow rise and plunge his weapon with all his force
into the monster's vitals. At first the animal strives
to escape, dragging the canoe after him ; but finding
that his enemies are close at his heels, he turns round
and rushes furiously at them with wide-open jaws.
The light boat dodges, backs, turns from right to left,
or skims away, with the dexterity of a trained horse
avoiding the charge of an elephant. One crunch of
the powerful jaws of the brute or one kick of his
foot crushes the frail craft into matchwork ; but the
hunters are prepared for such a catastrophe, and
instantly dive and swim under water to the shore

while their enemy is looking for them on the surface. Then another boat coming to the rescue carries on the contest, and the big water-horse succumbs at last from wounds and loss of blood.   "This hunting," says Livingstone, " is the bravest thing I ever saw."

The night is often made hideous by the shrieks of another of the strange denizens of these forests. This is the soko—either the gorilla which Du Chaillu saw on the Ogowai river, or a closely allied species of "wild-man-o'-the-woods." A glimpse was caught of this singular animal by Cameron on the Tanganyika; Stanley heard much about it while voyaging down the Lualaba ; but only Livingstone has given authentic particulars regarding it. Its true home of course is among the trees ; but it can make its way at considerable speed over the ground, using its long fore-arms as crutches, and "hitching" itself along on its knuckles. In many of its ways it is exceedingly human-like. Stanley describes their chattering and quarrelling among the branches as indistinguishable from the sound of natives squabbling ; to Lieutenant Cameron they looked like a company of black men, only bigger. He was told that they build a nest for themselves every night; but Livingstone says that these structures show no more science than a cushat's nest. The missionary tells, however, that the soko will pull out a spear, if it is stabbed with one, and stanch the wound with leaves or grass. He describes it as a hideous, pot-bellied creature, whose repulsiveness is increased by its wrinkled yellow face, human-like features, and incipient whiskers and beard. The soko, however, is not so bad as it looks. It will not, he says, attack an unarmed man or a woman, and only springs upon a person carrying a spear, from a fear that he is about to assault it. Its mode of attack is invariably to seize the intruder in its powerful arms, get his hand into its mouth, and one by one bite off his fingers and spit them out. It has been known to kidnap babies, and carry them up into the trees, but this seems to be more out of sport than mischief. In his family relations the male soko is a model of affection—assisting the mother to carry her young, and attending strictly to the proprieties of soko society. A young soko which was in the doctor's possession had many intelligent and winning ways; showed great affection and gratitude, was careful in making its bed and tucking itself in every night, and scrupulously wiped its nose with leaves. In short, it must be allowed that the native verdict that the "soko have good in him" is borne out by the known facts, and that in some respects he compares not unfavourably, both in character and manners, with some of the men we make acquaintance with in our wanderings through Africa.

Crossing the Chambesi, and climbing the northern slope of the valley, Livingstone, in the beginning of April 1867, found himself on the mountains overhanging a sheet of water called Lake Liemba, which subsequently turned out to be the southern end of our old acquaintance, Tanganyika. Thence his route zigzagged away to the westward, through a land full of swamps and slow-running streams, flowing

towards the setting sun. So saturated was the soil
with moisture, that for days solid land was not to
be found. Where there was not absolute swamp
and mire, the ground was covered with a matted
green carpet—a thin crust of vegetation and soil
covering "the waters under the earth"—which rose
and fell a foot at each step. These treacherous
places had to be crossed with a light step, and without pausing, for at the least delay the foot might
slip through the floating mass, and the unhappy
traveller plunge up to the armpits in mire.

In the spring of 1867, the reservoir which absorbed
the contents of this sponge-like tract was reached.
This was Lake Moero, a sheet of water almost insignificant for Central Africa, yet whose farther shore
was not visible, except on very clear days, to the
visitor to its coasts. A black wall of mountains
frowned on its western side, but elsewhere its banks
were flat. A broad, deep stream flowed into its
southern end, and escaped at its northern extremity
much enlarged in volume. Livingstone was told
that further to the north this great river—the
Lualaba—spread into a larger lake—Kamolondo—
about the point of its junction with a stream of
equal or even greater magnitude coming from the
south-westwards, named the Lufira, and that the
united waters continued their course to the northward through new lakes and unknown countries
occupied by wild and cannibal races. It was now
that Livingstone got his first hint that he was
working not, as he supposed, on the Zambesi, but

on some new river-system. He instantly rushed to
the conclusion that he was on the head-waters
of the great river of Egypt,—the wish no doubt
being father to the thought,—and up to his last day,
though doubts occasionally visited him that it was
the course of the despised Congo on which he had
lighted, he was firmly convinced that he was engaged
on the exploration of the hidden sources of the Nile.
He would fain have followed the river downwards
to the sea, but there was civil war ahead, and the
whole country was flooded; so he turned his steps
southwards in search of another great lake through
which the Lualaba was said to flow before reaching
Moero.

But, first, the great potentate of the region,
Cazembe, whose chief town was situated within a
few miles of the shores of Moero lake, had to be
visited. The importance and the splendour of
Cazembe's court were found to have been much
exaggerated. The chief held only an elective rule,
and his barbaric state was no greater than that of
scores of other black " kings" in Africa. He turned
out, however, to be a very friendly and hospitable
personage, in spite of his squinting eyes and generally sinister aspect, the row of human skulls with
which his gates were garnished, and the number of
his courtiers who had had their ears cropped and
their hands chopped off. The doctor did not want
for meal, meat, and fish, foaming pombe and banana
wine, so long as he stayed with Cazembe; but the
chief was in no hurry to part with his white guests,

CROSSING A SPONGE.

Page 151.

and put off as long as possible his promise to
supply guides to the unknown lake. But even
an African king will run short of excuses for delay,
and so on the 18th of July 1868 Dr. Livingstone
found himself, after several weeks' tramp through wet
and dry, on the rushy margin of Lake Bangweolo.

It is a grand expanse of water, this that had lain so
long hid in the inmost recesses of the dark continent
of Africa, though its shores have not the bold pictur-
esqueness of those of Tanganyika, or the rich diversity of those of the Victoria Nyanza. Close to the
spot where the discoverer came in sight of it, a wide
arm, gradually narrowing to a breadth of half a mile,
reached away to the northward. It was the outlet
of the lake, the great Lualaba, here known as the
Luapula. The lake itself lies east and west, is
oval in outline, and measures two hundred miles
in length, by about one hundred and thirty in
breadth. Vast tracts of flooded forest and marsh
surround the open water, especially on the eastern
and southern shores, and may almost be regarded as
forming part of the lake. The water is of a deep sea-
green colour, and rests on a bed of pure white sand.
No bold bluffs or fantastically coloured cliffs jut out
from the shores of Bangweolo. But for the scattered
villages of the fishermen, its surroundings would
have a depressing aspect of loneliness and monotony.
A few islands break the sky-line, and from these
others are visible nearer the centre of the lake.
Sailing out in a canoe to the farthest of these isles,
Livingstone saw on every side an ocean horizon.

Wide as was the view around him, he was never in all his lonely life in a more lonely spot—never so far beyond the ken of civilization.

Having ascertained that a range of mountains ran along the southern side of the lake, separating its water-shed from that of the Zambesi, and that the Chambesi river flowing into its eastern end was the head-waters of the Lualaba, the doctor retraced his steps to the north, and resolved to follow a new line of exploration. He would return to Tanganyika, and making to the north-westward, would strike the course of the Lualaba further down, and follow it until, as he hoped, he had proved it to be the Nile. Terrible trials and sufferings marked this journey. Impediments met him at every step; his illnesses returned upon him with fourfold force; his followers deserted him; his stores of food were exhausted; the natives were hostile and treacherous. For sixteen days he was carried in a litter, under the vertical rays of the sun, over rough hills and thorny and marshy hollows in which the water frequently mounted to the waists of the bearers. The road constantly rose and fell over the uneven boggy ground, and every jolt was torture to the sick and toilworn traveller. The sight of the Tanganyika revived for a little his drooping spirits; but still he feared that he must die ere he reached Ujiji, and then, he writes, "all the letters that await me will be useless." On the 14th of March 1869 he arrived at the goal for which he so despairingly longed, but found awaiting him no aid or supplies, no medicines, no letters. Mirambo was on the war-path against the Arabs, and the road to the coast was closed.

Slowly the traveller's strength returned; but several months elapsed before he found himself able to set out for the unknown country to the west through which the Lualaba flows after leaving Lake Kamolondo. Even the Arab slave-traders had not previously penetrated so far into the interior. Livingstone followed in the trail of these desperadoes, and saw but too abundant examples of their methods of "opening up" the country. Again, as he began to descend the slope towards the great river, he entered the region of forest, marsh, and running stream. The hill-sides were ploughed by the waters into deep ravines, some of them filled to the lips with the dense growth of trees and shrubs spread like a sombre green pall over the face of the land. Others of these *cañons* show steep cliff-like sides, draped with trailing mosses and ferns. This route has also been traversed by Cameron and Stanley, and their more detailed narrative bears out the description of Livingstone, which shows that a new region, markedly distinct in its plant and animal life, and in its races of men and their customs, is entered into so soon as the water-shed is crossed. In the very first country reached, Ubujwa, we meet with "caste," unknown to the eastern side of the continent, the upper classes being distinguished by tattooing and ornaments, as well as in dress and features, from those beneath them. Then follows a more mountainous country, Uvinza—a succession of sharp ridges separated by

profound gullies.   The eye cannot penetrate the
gloom of these abysses, and only a faint murmur of
waters tells that a river flows through their depths.
The only means of crossing them is often by a bridge
of ratans or the trunk of some fallen tree.   The
ridges can sometimes only be surmounted by clinging
to rocks and creepers, and scrambling like a squirrel
from branch to branch.   Often a decayed trunk
hangs threateningly over the head of the explorer,
kept upright by the parasitical plants that bind the
forest trees together like great cables. " Into these
primeval woods," says Livingstone, " the sun, though
vertical, cannot penetrate, except as sending down
their pencils of rays into the gloom.   The rain-water
stands for months in stagnant pools made by elephants' feet, and the dead leaves decay on the damp
soil.   One feels himself the veriest pigmy before
these gigantic trees; many of their roots, high out
of the soil in the path, keep you constantly looking
down, and a good gun does no harm to the parrots
and guinea-fowl on their tops.   The climbing plants,
from the size of a whipcord to that of a man-of-war's
hawser, make the ancient path the only passage."

Beyond the mountains we reach the great alluvial
plain, bordering on the Lualaba, occupied by a
strange race of people — the Manyuema.   Here
Livingstone passed many months: first in attempts
to reach the great river, the paths being closed by
the wars which the Arab inroad had stirred up; and
then at Nyangwe, on the Lualaba, in futile endeavours to continue his journey.   He mingled much with

the Manyuema, and found something in them to ad-
mire and a great deal to shock and disgust. They
are a fine race—the most handsome and athletic he
had seen in Africa. Some of the female Manyuema
especially might be described as beautiful in features
as well as form. They have made a good deal of
progress in the arts of agriculture and manufacture
as practised among savages. The country is thickly
peopled, large villages being met with at the end of
every mile or two of march. The houses are neatly
built, with red painted walls, thatched eaves, and
doorways higher than one is accustomed to see in
Africa ; and they are generally arranged on a regular
plan, the streets radiating from a central space.
The cottages are shaded by banana and other fruit
trees, and around the villages are large areas
planted with maize, manioc, sweet potatoes, yams,
and sesamum. The inhabitants are clever smiths,
tanners, and weavers. The chiefs are imposing-
looking personages, with dirks and sharp two-edged
swords stuck in their girdles, a permanent cone-
shaped cap, composed of their own hair plastered
with clay, in addition to a multiplicity of bangles,
rings, bells, and nose and ear ornaments. These
"superior persons" wear a kilt of grass-cloth, of a
gaudy tartan pattern, giving them a not remote resemblance to imperfectly dressed Rob Roys painted
black. The vulgar herd have generally to be content with a leathern apron. It seems only too well
established that these fine-looking fellows are cannibals. Livingstone was never able to obtain con-

clusive proof on the point, though the evidence
pointed strongly in that direction. He was of
opinion that it was only their captive enemies that
they ate, and that they had been led to the practice
by their indulgence in soko flesh. The soko, indeed,
they are inclined to regard as a member of the human
family; if not exactly one of ourselves, at least a
poor relation. At one of the Manyuema villages
Mr. Stanley noticed a row of one hundred and eighty-
six skulls decorating the principal streets, and was
told that they were remains of sokos, the trophies of
former feasts. He carried off two of the skulls, and
presented them to Professor Huxley, who declared
that they were negro craniums of the usual type.

Whether habitual cannibals or not, the Manyuema
have the most callous indifference for human suffering and bloodshed; and the slave-traders found it
the easiest task imaginable to set the tribes at each
other's throats. These ruffians having gained complete ascendency with their fire-arms, sided first
with one party and then with another, and when the
combatants were sufficiently weak they all fell an
easy prey. From his camp at Nyangwe Livingstone
counted at one time ten and at another seventeen
villages in flames at once. The slavers' depredations
culminated in a massacre of more than ordinary
atrocity.

One of the great institutions of the Manyuema
country is their markets, held in certain villages
and at stated times. Even in war-time market
people are allowed to pass freely to and from the

ASSEMBLING TO MARKET, NYANGWE.

Page 158.

fairs with their wares. People from distant districts collect here, and exchange their surplus products for Manyuema luxuries. Fish-wives, goat-
herds, slave-owners; dealers in ivory, palm oil,
pottery, skins, cloth, and iron-ware; sellers of fruit,
vegetables, salt, grain, and fowls, all mingle in the
motley throng, and shout the merits of their particular goods at the top of their lungs, and with
a perseverance and ardour that would make the
fortune of an auctioneer at home. Strange varieties
of savage costume and no costume are to be seen in
these groups: the wild Balegga man-eater stalking
side by side with the white-skirted Moslem man-
hunter from Zanzibar; and the plumed, painted,
tattooed, and bespangled chieftain laying his dignity
temporarily aside to chaffer with a poor commoner
in his simple waistcloth, over the price of a pig or
of a mess of roasted white ants. At Nyangwe there
was a market once in every four days, and the
assemblage generally numbered about three thousand.
One fair-day the Arabs, who had been sauntering
peaceably among the crowd, suddenly produced their
arms and began firing on the helpless multitude,
chiefly composed of women. Flinging down their
wares, the panic-stricken people fled on all sides,
many of them dashing into the river that flowed
close by, or climbing into boats that filled and sank
with the numbers that crowded into them. The
market-place was strewn with the dead and dying,
and with the confused heaps of merchandise which
had been dropped or thrown down in the flight,

while the murderous scoundrels continued firing so
long as they could see a victim to aim at.

Livingstone believed that five hundred lives were
sacrificed in this unprovoked massacre. The object
was to "strike terror" into the hearts of the inhabitants, and show them the irresistible power of the
gun. The result was that the country became too
hot to hold the murderers. Livingstone, rather than
continue to be a witness of their monstrous crimes,
resolved to abandon his attempt to continue his
journey. He had learned a good deal at Nyangwe
of the course and character of the Lualaba, but he
still believed that it was the Nile. At this point the
river is a full mile in breadth, flowing north-westwards with a deep rapid current of a pale gray tint,
between low banks, and sprinkled over with little
green islands covered with sedge and trees. Some
distance below, a great tributary, the Lomame, falls
into it on the opposite bank. The main stream of
the Lualaba, Livingstone was told, was not the branch
which he had traced between Lake Bangweolo and
Lake Moero, but another river, rising in a chain of
mountains in the south, which joins it in Lake
Kamolondo. The inhabitants on this stream lived
in strange underground dwellings,—galleries and
chambers excavated in the soil or chiselled out of
the rocks. Near its head were copper-workings,
and its source was in a fountain on a rounded hill,
from a spring in which also flowed the Lomame;
while on its southern side were the head-springs of
the Zambesi, and of its chief tributary, the Kafue.

MARKET IN MANYUEMA.

Page 559.

" The Mountains of the Moon!" was the doctor's mental note, " the hills Crophi and Mophi! the Fountains of the Nile! the ancient Mines of Copper! the Troglodytes! Here they all are, just where Ptolemy and other venerable authorities placed them; and other explorers, who are wandering astray in search of them to the northward, have turned their backs on the true beginnings of the sacred river of Egypt." And in this firm belief he ceased from seeking to follow up the Lualaba, and turning his own back upon the sources of the Nile, resisting the entreaties of Stanley, and the natural longings of his heart to revisit home, he followed what he was persuaded was the marked-out path of duty, leading him to the enigmatical fountains which he had heard of among the savages of Manyuema. Cameron, the next comer to that country, was told quite a different tale by those accomplished fictionists; and, by means which were not in Livingstone's power, he proved that the Lualaba could not be the Nile, for the two simple reasons, that its volume was many times larger, and its level many hundred feet lower, than that of the White Nile at Gondokoro.

After two years of absence, the veteran missionary was again at Ujiji, where Stanley was one of the first to greet him. Other dangers besides sickness and privation had beset him; for the country was up in arms, the avengers of blood were at his heels, having confounded him with the strangers who were desolating the land, and twice in one day he had narrow escapes from spears hurtling close past him

(658)　　　　　14

from the thicket. Another year passed before new
stores reached him from the coast and he was able
to set out on his final journey. This last sad chapter
of the story of a noble life is a record of suffering
borne with heroic patience and steadfastness rather
than a narrative of exploration and adventure, and
it may be swiftly passed over.

The start was from Unyanyembe, on the 14th
of August 1872; the route lay along the eastern
side of Tanganyika, and round the northern,
eastern, and southern shores of Bangweolo. From
the first a full share of the hardships and discouragements of African travel fell to their lot,
but it was not till they began the long descent
into the hollow, at the bottom of which lies Bangweolo, that the misery and gloom began to accumulate with more than ordinary intensity. The rain
fell incessantly. The path was a miry track, between
high walls of dripping grass and cane, in which the
foot slipped and sank at every step. The spongy
soil had soon soaked up all the moisture it could
contain, but still the skies poured down a pitiless
flood on the drowned land. The country was flat,
with no hillock or rock from which the travellers
could catch a glimpse of their surroundings, or see a
way of escape from their difficulties. The way they
followed, sloping imperceptibly to the lake level, led
them deeper into the mire and mud. Every mile or
two a river had to be crossed,—a sluggish, turbid
stream, with a wide margin of inundated marsh on
either bank. It was impossible to tell where the

river merged into the swamp, and the swamp into the land.

Still the forlorn band plodded slowly on, skirting as closely as possible the northern coast of the lake, and seeking a way round its eastern end. "Rain! rain! rain!" is the doctor's entry on Christmas day. At the close of January there was no cessation of the downfall; it seemed as if it would never fair. The malarial fever again seized on the explorer with re-doubled force. He who had in earlier years always marched briskly at the head of his men, now dragged his limbs wearily in the rear. Sometimes he was able to keep his seat on one of the asses that accom-panied his train; but at other times this exertion was too painful, and he staggered feebly along with the support of two of his faithful men. He was no longer able to wade the streams, and had to be car-ried through the muddy currents on the shoulders of his servants. The toil and misery of these cross-ings may be imagined from the fact that the water occasionally rose to the chins of the bearers, and that they were liable at any moment to plunge into deep holes or become firmly entangled in the mud and weeds. The surrounding country was uninhabited—indeed, uninhabitable. The supplies of food began to fail, and hunger was added to the torments of the march. The guides deserted, and the fated band struggled on through fen and brake, not knowing whither they were journeying, seeing nothing from day to day save the tall, damp barriers of jungle that hemmed them in, and the gloomy sky overhead.

The Chambesi river—here three hundred yards wide and three fathoms deep—was, however, found and crossed, and the wanderers began to turn their faces westward along the south side of Bangweolo. The doctor was able to walk no further; when he climbed upon his ass, he fell to the ground from sheer weakness. His devoted retainers—Chouma, Susi, Jacob Wainwright, and the others—carried him by turns on their shoulders, or in a litter which they constructed. On the 23rd of April and the three following days he was able only to write in his diary the date, and the distances marched—from a mile to two miles and a half. On the 27th occurs the last entry, waveringly traced with his dying hand: " Knocked up quite, and remain—recover—sent to buy milch goats. We are on the banks of the R[iver] Molilamo." His last day's march, like so many that had gone before, was partly through the interminable marsh and in rain. His bearers had to halt often, so violent were his pains and so great his exhaustion. Arrived at the village of Chitambo, in Ilala, he was helped from the litter to the bed of leaves spread for him in a native hut. He spoke kindly to his humble companions, and asked anxiously how many days' march it was to the Lualaba. The malarial poison was already, however, exercising its benumbing power over his faculties; even the fountains of the Nile had faded into dimness, if not into utter darkness, before his mind's eye.

In the morning of the 1st of May the servant set to watch by him awoke and found his master

kneeling by the side of his rude couch in an atti-
tude of prayer. Alarmed by the utter stillness of
the figure, he called in his companions. The brave
spirit had fought its last fight in the darkness, and
had fled. The noble Christian philanthropist, the
manful champion of the weak and oppressed, the un-
wearied and keen-eyed lover of nature, the intrepid
explorer whose name is as inseparably connected
with Africa as that of Columbus is with America,
had sunk down exhausted in the very heart of the
continent, with his life-long work still unfinished.
His highest praise is that he spent thirty years in the
darkest haunts of cruelty and savagery and yet
never shed the blood of his fellow-man. The noblest
testimony to his character and his influence is the
conduct of that faithful band of native servants who
had followed his fortunes so long and so far, and who,
embalming his body, and secretly preserving all his
papers and possessions, carried safely back over the
long weary road to the coast all that remained of
the hero and his work.

CHAPTER III.

CATARACTS AND CANNIBALS.

" The long day wanes ; the slow moon climbs ; the deep
Moans round with many voices. Come, my friends,
'Tis not too late to seek a newer world.
Push off, and sitting well in order, smite
The sounding furrows ; for my purpose holds
To sail beyond the sunset, and the baths
Of all the western stars, until I die.
It may be that the gulfs will wash us down ;
It may be we will touch the Happy Isles."

TENNYSON, *Ulysses.*

WHILE Livingstone was lingering for so
many months on the banks of the Lua-
laba at Nyangwe, he looked daily with
eager longing at the strong, deep, mile-
broad current that swept placidly past and disappeared into the depths of the unexplored continent.
Behind, to the eastward, lay eight hundred miles of
the breadth of Africa which had already been crossed ;
but ahead there stretched nearly a thousand miles of
absolutely unknown country between him and the
Atlantic. Into that ocean, a thousand miles in a
straight line west-south-west of his present position,
the Congo discharged itself, and its stream, pouring
apparently from the central reservoir, had been traced

for one hundred and fifty miles from the coast. But
this Lualaba flowed almost due north, as if heading
for the Nile or the Niger. He longed for the power
to embark on its waters, and follow its mysterious
fortunes to the "bitter end," whether in the Mediterranean or the Western Sea. But he had to give
up the idea as fool-hardy. The shaggy forests that
covered the land in front were even more gloomy and
forbidding than those that lay behind; the tribes
that haunted their depths were ferocious and untamed to an extent that made the Manyuema seem
mild and civilized by comparison. No volunteers
could be found rash enough to brave the known and
the unknown dangers of the route; and for an explorer to venture upon this wild enterprise weakly
guarded was to court certain destruction. Cameron
also found the difficulties of following the course of
the Lualaba insuperable, and bent his steps to the
south-westward instead. Stanley, however, who
arrived here in the close of 1876, was differently situated. Not a whit behind his predecessors in courage
and energy, he possessed what they wanted—money
—which has an almost absolute power even in Central Africa—and men. His followers, in spite of all
the losses of the expedition, still numbered about one
hundred and forty. The weaklings had been weeded
out by the toils and troubles of the journey; those
that remained were now veterans, trained in a hard
school to obedience and steadfastness. The best assurance of their fidelity was the fact that if they deserted
they would infallibly be killed, and probably eaten.

The American explorer made the great resolve to dare all—to join his life and fortunes to this river, and like his countryman's bull-terrier, as recorded by Mark Twain, " kinder freeze to it," until he found its outlet.

So he marshalled his people, his captains of tens and fifties, with the women and children of his force, and addressed them in pithy and stirring words, like a Viking or some other old-world warrior about to lead his men on some desperate adventure where glory and peril would be reaped in equal proportions. The answer was not lukewarm, and they set out from Manyuema, plunging at once into the abysses of the virgin forest. Such woods, so tall and dense and sombre, the traveller had never before invaded. Compared with them the forests of Uganda and along the shores of Tanganyika seemed mere jungle and thicket. Even the Manyuema had penetrated but a little way into their depths. They line the course of the Lualaba on both sides for fifteen hundred miles below Nyangwe, and stretch back from its banks to unknown distances. Ahead of Stanley's expedition went a large party of Arabs and their retainers from the coast—some seven hundred in number—whom he had hired as his escort for the first stages of the journey. The long file extended for miles along the narrow elephant track, and frequent halts had to be made to cut a path through the thicket, or to rest the weary carriers.

" The trees," says the explorer, " kept shedding their dews upon us like rain in great round drops. Every leaf seemed weeping. Down the boles and branches, creepers and vegetable cords, the moisture trickled and fell on us. Overhead the wide-spreading branches, in many interlaced strata, each branch heavy with broad, thick leaves, absolutely shut out daylight. We knew not whether it was a sunshiny day or a dull foggy day, for we marched in a feeble solemn twilight, such as you experience in temperate climes an hour after sunset. It was so dark sometimes that I could not see the words recording notes of the track which I pencilled in my note-book. To right and left, to the height of about twenty feet, towered the undergrowth,—the lower world of vegetation. What rude blast can visit these imprisoned shades? The tempest might roar without the leafy world, but in its deep bosom there is absolute stillness."

Every few hundred yards the path dived down into the bed of a swampy water-course or ravine filled with water-plants and festooned with tough creepers, armed some of them with formidable hooks that cut the bare feet and exposed limbs of the porters to the bone. It soon became almost impossible to force a way through this dense mass of vegetation for the unwieldy sections of the *Lady Alice*, which after her many wanderings by land and sea was about to start on a more perilous voyage than any that had preceded. The Arabs, too, had soon enough of the forest life, for sickness was striking down their men in scores. It was resolved to take to the river, and face the dangers from the

numerous rapids and the savage cannibal tribes on
its shores, rather than continue to struggle through
these thorny and gloomy shades.

The river-margin was reached, the *Lady Alice* put
together and launched, and the voyage down-stream
began, a land party following the river-bank parallel
with the boat. The stream and the dwellers thereon
were not long in each giving a taste of their peculiar
quality. A dangerous rapid had to be shot down.
The natives swarmed out in their canoes, uttering wild
war-whoops. The passage of the river became one long
running fight between the spear and arrow and the
musket. So soon as the boat made its appearance
round a bend of the stream, the kettle-drums gave
the alarm in the native villages, and soon the great
war-horns and war-drums boomed out their deep
notes across the waters. The savages rushed to their
canoes, and paddled out gleefully to intercept the
strangers, of whom they expected to make an easy prey.
It was evident from their shouts and gestures that
they were in search not merely of spoil but of supper.
No doubt was left in the minds of Stanley and his
crew, from the ghastly remains of human feasts in
their villages, that the tribes on this part of the Lualaba, and for many hundreds of miles below, are cannibals of the most pronounced and ferocious type.
If the *Lady Alice* found it impossible to escape by
speed from her enemies, the tactics often adopted
were to moor her in the stream, raise a bulwark of
captured shields above her gunwale, and behind this
barrier, impervious to arrow or spear, await the

attack. Sometimes the first discharge of musketry put the assailants to ignominious flight. More frequently the battle was prolonged for hours, though it invariably ended in the assailants being beaten off. Stanley did not, of course, stop to collect statistics of his victories; but the number of the savages killed in these fights must have been something considerable. The members of the expedition, protected though they were, did not come off lightly. At the end of the first month over twenty "naval engagements" had been fought, and not thirty of the party had escaped wounds. Many seats were empty, the owners having fallen victims to the river, to the cunning enemy, or to small-pox and other diseases that attacked the expedition with great virulence.

The land party fared even worse. Darts were launched upon them from the thickets, and ambuscades lay in wait for them at every turn. From the "Expedition Camp" relief parties had to be sent to their help, and to guide them when, as often happened, they lost their way. The difficulties of the forest path became, if possible, greater as they proceeded; the unhealthy, steaming atmosphere seemed to thicken and the dripping branches to be more closely interwoven, until they had to burrow and crawl on hands and feet through the tangle like wild animals. The Arabs had had enough of it. They refused to proceed further, though they were still eight days' march from the point agreed upon for parting company; and Stanley and his men were left alone in the wilderness.

Something must be resolved upon, and quickly.

otherwise nothing could save the expedition. A cannibal tribe had, as usual, attacked the boat, and had
been beaten to an island in mid-stream, where their
boats were drawn up. By a brilliant stratagem, carried out by the leader and his faithful Frank Pocock,
the enemy's boats were "cut out" during the night
and towed to the shore. Peace negotiations were
then entered into with the savages, resulting in
twenty-two canoes being retained by the explorers
as indemnity; and in these the whole of the expedition, with their goods and chattels, embarked on the
28th December 1876, the *Lady Alice* showing the
way down-stream, and the crews responding with
hearty shouts to the declaration of the leader that
they should "toil on and on by this river and no
other to the salt sea."

The tom-toming, the blasts of the war-horns, the
incessant attacks of the cannibals went on from day
to day, till even the fighting became monotonous. The
safety of the party lay in the width of the great
stream, which enabled them to move to whichever
bank seemed most deserted, or keep in mid-river
if attacks were threatened from both sides. Tributaries, each of them a mighty stream, discharged
themselves into the Lualaba, and increased its breadth
and volume. One of these was the Lomame, or
Young's river, coming from Livingstone's supposed
" Fountains" in the south, and which is six hundred
yards wide at the mouth, and flows between low
banks densely covered with timber. But the chief
affluents are on the right bank of the Lualaba. Of

these the Luama is four hundred yards wide, the Lira three hundred yards only, but of great depth, and the Urindi five hundred yards; but they are puny streams beside the Lowwa, which is two-thirds of a mile broad at its junction with the main river. Still further down, and also on the north bank, the Mbura discharges itself into the Lualaba by two branches, each two hundred yards in breadth; and a hundred and fifty miles lower down there is suddenly opened the vast mouth of the Aruwimi, two thousand yards from shore to shore, and leading, like a broad highway, to regions still unvisited.

Ere this point is reached strange vicissitudes have occurred to the river itself and to the voyagers on it. The breadth of the stream has increased from two thousand to three thousand and latterly four thousand yards. Its course has been persistently northward. The Equator has been reached, but still the direction of the Lualaba corresponds with that of the Nile Valley. Can it be, thinks the leader of the little flotilla, that Livingstone was right, and that this after all is the Nile? He had little time for reflection, so unremitting were the natives in their attentions, and so desperately hard was the toil of working down-stream. Just below the mouth of the Lomane begin a series of cataracts—seven of them within a distance of seventy miles—with roaring rapids between, where the Lualaba cuts its way through a range of hills as it descends from a higher to a lower level in its bed. The channel is contracted to a third or even a sixth of its ordinary breadth, and through this narrow gorge the stream tumbles and boils, flinging itself over ledges of rock, or dashing frantically against the walls that hem it in, as if it were struggling with all its giant power to escape from its prison. Within the gorge the ear is stunned with the continual din of the rushing waters, and the attention kept constantly on the strain to avoid the perils of rock, rapid, whirlpool, and cataract with which the course is strewn. With extreme caution and good-luck the rapids may be run in safety; but how are frail canoes to survive the experiment of a plunge over a perpendicular ledge, in company with millions of tons of falling water, into an abyss of seething and gyrating foam?

On shore the dangers are scarcely less formidable than on the water. The cannibal natives lie in wait to oppose the landing, or better still, to slay or capture victims wherewith to replenish their larders. A toilsome ascent has to be made to the summit of the bluffs forming the river-banks over rough boulders and through tangled forest. In places where the fall of the stream is slight it may be possible to lower down the boats, by means of strong hawsers of creepers, to the pool below; but in other cases the canoes have to be dragged painfully up the cliffs, and launched again with almost equal toil where the current seems a little calmer. All this while the poisoned arrows are hissing through the air, spears are launched out of every thicket where a wily savage can find a hiding-place, and stones are slung or thrown at the unlucky

pioneers from each spot of vantage ground. Only by
stationing van and rear guards and flanking parties,
and maintaining a brisk fire on the bush, can the
assailants be kept at bay. When a camp is formed
for the night, the wearied members of the expedition,
after posting a strong guard, hope for a little rest
after the terrible trials of the day. Most likely they
are disappointed. The vindictive assailants never
leave off exhibiting proofs of their hostility during the
whole night ; and the whiz of the flying arrows, the
hurtling of lances through the stockade, and the sharp
crack of the rifle mingle with the dreams of the sleeper.

One morning at day-break it was found that
the savage fishermen had spread their nets all
about the camp, and were waiting outside, expecting
to make a great haul. The expedition broke through
this and all the other toils drawn round it ; but each
day there were new labours to begin and new attacks
to be beaten off. Sometimes prisoners were made ;
but so low was the intelligence of the natives, and so
inveterate their animosity, that hardly any progress
could be made in this way towards a peaceable
understanding. One curious prize fell into the hands
of the strangers—a member of a tribe of dwarfs, the
Watwa, who inhabit the country some distance up
the Lomane. He was only four and a half feet high
—a miserable object—bow-legged and thin-shanked,
with a straggling fringe of whisker round his ape-
like features, whose appearance aroused no consum-
ing desire that pigmies should be more common in the
world than they are.

The descent of the Stanley Falls, as this region of
cataracts and cannibals has been named, was not
accomplished by the expedition without loss of life
and property. In spite of every precaution, canoes
would be dragged from their moorings and be sucked
down by the whirlpools or swept over the falls; or
the occupants would lose nerve in the presence of
danger, and allow their craft to drift into the powerful centre current, whence escape was hopeless. One
marvellously narrow escape there was. A canoe was
capsized in a piece of bad water, just above one of
the falls. Two of the three men on board swam to
the shore; the third, clinging to his boat, was carried
straight towards the cataract. Luckily, a few feet
from the brink of the fall, a single pointed rock pro-
jected from the bed of the stream. On this the canoe
struck, and one side getting jammed below the surface, the other tilted up. To this frail hold the luck-
less man clung, with his feet dipping in the water,
and hanging, as it were, on the verge of eternity.
Numerous were the devices adopted by his comrades
to rescue him from his doom. Ropes were flung
towards him, and attempts made to float empty
canoes within his reach, but to no effect. At length
a canoe, with two bold spirits on board—one of whom
was Uledi, the coxswain of the expedition, who by
pluck and coolness was instrumental in saving a score
of lives during the descent of the Lualaba—essayed
the dangerous task. Stout cables were lashed to bow
and stern, and were held by the strong hands of men
on the shore, and by this means the boat was guided

towards its goal. When within ten yards of the terrified wretch, a rope was flung to him, and clutching at it he disappeared over the falls into the yawning gulf below. The canoe drifted against a rocky islet that divided the falls, and on pulling the rope it was discovered that the drowning man was still at the end of it, and he was hauled safely to the little isle. It seemed but reprieve from death, and night fell before anything could be done to effect a rescue. But next morning the means were found to float cables to the rock, where the three men maintained a precarious foothold, and one by one they were dragged hand over hand through the raging current. Simultaneously, however, another canoe had been upset, and one man was carried down into the chasm to certain death.

After twenty-two days of incessant labour, the expedition once more floated in smooth waters below the Stanley Falls. The banks of the stream again opened up, and its breadth spread out to a mile or a mile and a half. At the same time the river suddenly changed its northerly direction to a course west-north-west. Before the Aruwimi is reached, the vast stream rolls between banks four thousand yards apart, and green fertile islands are sprinkled on its broad bosom. No change, however, is manifest in the character of the natives of its banks. If possible, they are more inveterately hostile and bloodthirsty than ever, and the most formidable attack yet made on the expedition occurred at the junction of the Aruwimi. The shores of both streams resounded to

the din of the everlasting war-drums, and from every
cove and island swarmed a crowd of canoes, that
began forming into line to intercept and attack the
travellers. These crafts were larger than any that
had yet been encountered. The leading canoe of the
savages was of portentous length, with forty paddlers
on each side, while on a platform at the bow were
stationed ten redoubtable young warriors, with
crimson plumes of the parrot stuck in their hair, and
poising long spears. Eight steersmen were placed on
the stern, with large paddles ornamented with balls of
ivory; while a dozen others, apparently chiefs, rushed
from end to end of the boat directing the attack.
Fifty-two other vessels of scarcely smaller dimensions
followed in its wake. From the bow of each waved a
long mane of palm fibre; every warrior was decorated
with feathers and ornaments of ivory; and the sound
of a hundred horns carved out of elephants' tusks,
and a song of challenge and defiance chanted from
two thousand savage throats, added to the wild excitement of the scene.

The assailants were put to flight after a series
of charges more determined and prolonged than usual.
This time, however, the blood of the strangers was
fully up. They were tired of standing everlast-
ingly on the defensive, of finding all their advances
repelled with scorn and hatred. They carried the
war into the enemy's camp, and drove them out of
their principal village into the forest. In the centre
of the village was found a singular structure—a
temple of ivory, the circular roof supported by thirty-

three large tusks, and surmounting a hideous idol,
four feet high, dyed a bright vermilion colour, with
black eyes, beard, and hair. Ivory here was "abundant as fuel," and was found carved into armlets,
balls, mallets, wedges, grain pestles, and other articles
of ornament and use; while numerous other weapons
and implements of iron, wood, hide, and earthenware
attested the ingenuity of the people. Their cannibal
propensities were as plainly shown in the rows of
skulls that grinned from poles, and the bones and
other grisly remains of human feasts scattered about
the village streets.

Collecting their spoils, the voyagers made haste to
leave the neighbourhood of the Aruwimi. Native
report spoke of great lake-like expansions higher up
the stream, and some day it may be one of the chief
highways to the heart of Africa. If it should turn
out to be, as Stanley has no hesitation in pronouncing
it, the Wellé of Schweinfurth, there is especial interest
attached to its exploration; for the Wellé, which from
its north-westerly course was supposed by the German
discoverer to flow into Lake Chad, passes through
a region of unique natural features and marvellous
beauty, inhabited by races, such as the Akka dwarfs
and the Nyam Nyam cannibals, that present some
marked points of difference from other African
peoples. Had we followed in the footsteps of Dr.
Schweinfurth, we would have seen him received
by the dignified King Munza of Monbuttu, in a lofty
and spacious hall, thronged with warriors and counsellors of state, some of them full-bearded, light-com-

plexioned men, with long, hooked Jewish noses,
wearing gorgeous vestments of fig-tree bark, copper
rings and chains, great cylindrical caps of papyrus
surmounted by plumes of ostrich and parrot, and
with sickle-like swords of gleaming copper girt to
their waists. But any one who desires to penetrate
to this region by the Aruwimi must obviously be
prepared to carry things with the high hand.

Below the Aruwimi the breadth of the main stream
continues to increase as it bends north-westerly to
the fourth degree of north latitude, then westerly,
and at last south-westwards to its outlet in the
Atlantic. Countless jungle-overgrown islands impede
its course, and between these it flows in numerous
channels, with a distance of from four to as many as
ten miles separating its opposing banks. For one
thousand miles the river is uninterrupted by rapids or
cataracts, and this portion of the voyage was in many
ways the most pleasant and peaceable. The shore-
dwellers were still frequently hostile, but the explorers
could now dodge them successfully out and in among
the islands, or slip past unobserved down some of the
central passages. At night the camp was pitched on
some secluded isle in mid-stream, where they could
sleep undisturbed by the fear of being made into a
stew ere morning. These little clumps of verdure
were full of botanical treasures,—fruit and oil-bear-
ing palms of many varieties, gaudy tropical flowers,
tall cotton-wood and teak trees, twining coils of
ratan and wild vine, and broad-leaved aquatic
plants; and though their shades were haunted by

myriads of mosquitoes that swarmed out and industriously drew toll from the veins of the passers-by,
though a dip in the stream was rendered dangerous
by the legions of crocodiles that lurked in its waters,
and the storms that often swept across the wide
reaches of the stream raised heavy brown waves that
threatened to swamp the canoes, the travellers had
been so harshly disciplined in the school of adversity
that these were counted as trifling discomforts.

It was only a respite, however, for worse dangers
and difficulties than any they had passed still lay
ahead; and though the breadth of the stream rendered
its navigation safe, it interfered with the objects of
exploration. They could never positively tell whether
the broad channels they saw opened up from time to
time were new tributaries of the Congo, or merely
passages between the islands. Those on the north
side might even have been branches thrown off by the
main stream to form the great Ogowai River, whose
upper course, in spite of the efforts of Du Chaillu,
Marche, Compiègne, Savorgnan de Brazza, and other
French explorers, is still little known. One great
affluent of the Congo, however, made its presence
unmistakably known. This is the Ikelemba, a river
not much over one thousand yards wide at its mouth,
but pouring a deep, impetuous torrent of dark, tea-
coloured water into the main stream. The volume of
water which it brings down is not greatly surpassed
by the giant Aruwimi and Lowwa combined. Below
the junction its dark-brown waters spread over a
breadth of three thousand yards, while the whity-

gray waves of the Congo are confined to the remaining five thousand yards, and thus the two streams flow side by side in the same bed without mingling, the divisional line plainly marked by a zigzag ripple for a distance of one hundred and thirty miles. The Ikelemba is reported by the natives to flow from a great unvisited lake, which is believed to be the same as one that Livingstone heard of at Nyangwe, and named Lake Lincoln. Further on, another large tributary of the Lualaba, or Congo, flows in—the Ibari-Nkutu, identical with the Kwango whose head-waters had been crossed by Livingstone and Cameron eight hundred miles to the southward.

By this time we have approached close to the western verge of the great central table-land, and are little more than four hundred miles from the coast of the Atlantic. For the last nine hundred miles the fall in the river-level has only been three hundred and sixty-four feet, and a descent of eleven hundred and fifty feet has still to be made ere the sea is reached. The days of smooth sailing are near an end, but fortunately also the natives have suddenly become peacefully and even helpfully disposed. Indications of intercourse with Europeans had been noticed some time before. The piratical Bangala tribe, that live near the mouth of the Ikelemba, are armed with old-fashioned muskets and clothed in cloth from the Manchester looms, which they had obtained by exchange from traders on the coast, the goods being handed on from one native market to another far into the interior of Africa. A furious assault was made on the strangers from the east coast; but the Snider was more than a match for the venerable flint-lock, and they passed on their way victoriously. At the Ibari-Nkutu, mountain spurs come down to the shores, the river narrows as precipitous cliffs take the place of the low, wooded banks, and then it opens up into a wide oval pool, walled in by chalk crags, reminding two of the voyagers—Stanley and his faithful assistant Frank Pocock—of the white coasts of England at Dover. At the lower end of the pool a hoarse, distant roar smote on their ears —familiar also, but of far other significance. The cataracts had begun again!

The next two hundred miles formed the most tedious, the most laborious, and the most disastrous portion of the river voyage, which had already lasted four months. The vast stream of the Lualaba-Congo, contracted to a breadth of twelve hundred yards, and often less, tore its way in foam and tumult through the gap which it has worn in the course of ages through the successive barriers of the coast ranges. In all this distance there are but few yards of smooth water. Reefs, narrows, rapids, cataracts, whirlpools, boiling caldrons succeed each other in seemingly endless succession. The rock and river scenery of these Livingstone Cataracts is an exaggeration of that of the Stanley Falls higher up. The cliffs lining the river are at first six hundred feet in height, but soon they tower to an altitude of from twelve hundred to fifteen hundred feet above the stream. Between them and the furious torrent there frequently inter-

poses only piled-up masses of boulder, over which it
is next to impossible to scramble. Sometimes the
tortured waters boil and roar at the very feet of the
perpendicular crags, and there is no passage except
by climbing up the face of the cliffs at some access-
ible spot, or trusting oneself to the tender mercies
of the stream. Stanley was often forced to adopt
this dangerous course, and twice at least he was
against his will shot like an arrow down a dangerous
rapid, narrowly shaving the rocks that jut up in all
parts of the river-bed.

Between the Ntamo Falls, the first of the Livingstone series, and the great Yellala Falls, which are
the last on the course of the river, no fewer than
thirty cataracts have to be descended. In general
these are not, like the Niagara Falls, or the Victoria
Falls on the Zambesi, deep leaps of the river over a
perpendicular ledge, but rather a succession of head-
long rushes, as if the stream were tearing down a
series of huge staircases. Stanley's vivid account of
the Great Ntamo Fall may stand for all.

"Take," he says, "a strip of sea, blown over by a
hurricane, four miles in length by half a mile in
breadth, and a pretty accurate conception of its rushing waves may be obtained. Some of the troughs
were one hundred yards in length, and from one to
another the mad river plunged. There was first a
rush down into the middle of an immense trough, and
then, by sheer force, the enormous volume would lift
itself upwards steeply until, gathering itself into a
ridge, it suddenly hurled itself twenty or thirty feet

straight upwards before rolling down into another trough. The roar was deafening and tremendous. I can only compare it to the thunder of an express train through a rock tunnel. To speak to my neighbour I had to bawl in his ear."

In this wild current, rushing along at a speed of thirty miles an hour, the most powerful ocean steamer would, he says, be as helpless as a cockleboat; and for the frail canoes, of course, there was no alternative but to drag them over rock and boulder to a point below the falls, or lift them bodily up to the level of the table-land that overhung the water. This fifteen hundred feet of sheer ascent involved almost incredible toil and long detours; and when the summit had been reached, a path had to be cut for the canoes through the unpruned forest and jungle. Frequently canoes were swept away by the stream and wrecked, and then a halt had to be made until trees were cut down and new vessels had been painfully hewn and fashioned out of the solid wood. Little time or temptation had the pioneers to linger and enjoy the sublime scenery of the terrific gorge. Yet, environed though they were on every side by perils and difficulties, their frames enfeebled by toil and fever, and their ears stunned by the constant roar of falling waters, it was impossible sometimes not to pause in breathless admiration of the tremendous prospects of crag and waterfall that opened up before them. Such a spot is that where the Edwin Arnold River flings itself, in one bound of three hundred feet, into the main stream, clearing the base of the cliffs by a distance of ten yards. Still more grand is the view at the entrance of the Nkenké, which rushes down from a height of one thousand feet in one enormous cascade; while close by it another stream takes a sheer plunge of four hundred feet into the river. "The noise of the Nkenké torrent," says Stanley, "resembled the roar of an express train over a railway bridge; that of Cataract River, taking its leap from the cliffs, was like the rumble of thunder; the last line of rapids, with its fretting and fuming flanks, was heard only as the swash of waves against a ship's prow when driven by a spanking breeze against a cross sea; while the cataract below lent its dull boom to swell the chorus of angry waters."

Many were the gaps made in the already thinned ranks of the expedition in struggling through this fatal "Valley of the Shadow." In one day Stanley saw three of his canoes with eleven of his men carried over a cataract and disappear in the wild whirl of waters below. First a boat, in which was Kalulu, the explorer's follower in two great expeditions, and the hero of a tale of African adventure which he wrote, was sucked within the power of the fall, and plunged sheer down into the abyss, from which neither it nor its occupants were seen to emerge. Hardly had the horror-stricken onlookers turned their eyes away from this calamity, when another canoe, with two men on board, was seen shooting swiftly down the centre stream towards what appeared certain death. By almost a miracle, however, they

DEATH OF FRANK POCOCK.   Page 187.

hit a spot where they made an "easy fall" over the ledge, and succeeded in struggling safely to land. Close behind came a third canoe, in which was only one man, driving to its fate. As the stern of the little craft tilted up, and the bow dived down over the edge of the fall, the boatman rose to his feet and shouted a farewell to his companions on the shore. No doubt was entertained of his fate, until a few days after he suddenly reappeared in the camp. He had been picked up insensible by the aborigines some distance down the stream, and had been kept by them a prisoner till he had found means to regain his freedom.

At another cataract the carpenter of the expedition was swept away and drowned. But the darkest day for the leader was that in which the last of his three white companions, the cheery and devoted Frank Pocock, was snatched from him by the remorseless waters. Pocock had been disabled by fever and by ulcers on his feet, and had been left behind with the rear of the party while the others carried the boats past the Massasse Falls. Chafing at the delay, and at the idea of being carried by natives, he got into a boat along with three companions, and insisted on making the mad attempt to "shoot" the falls. The certain result followed. The boat capsized, and was sucked down into the vortex below the cataract. It emerged again, and the three black men, clinging to its keel, were floated to a place of safety. But poor young Pocock, courageous and powerful swimmer though he was, found his last

(e:s) 16

resting-place in one of the profoundest pools of the deep Congo.

Miserable weeks of unavailing grief, of vexing delays, of insubordination and desertion among his followers, of trouble with the natives of the country, and of ceaseless toil, followed for Stanley; but at last he struggled clear of all the impediments of the river, and marched, the gaunt, tattered, and prematurely gray-haired leader of a hungry and haggard band, across the open country to Boma, where, as he knew, there were European oil factories and plantations and English residents. There, among men of his own race, surrounded by civilized comforts to which he had long been a stranger, he soon forgot the toils and perils he had passed through in the natural elation at having accomplished an exploit almost unparalleled in the history of adventure.

On the 12th of August 1877, three years after the start from the Indian Ocean, eight months from setting out from Nyangwe to follow the Lualaba, the expedition emerged from the broad portal of the Congo into the Atlantic. They could hardly themselves believe that this vast flood, pouring two million cubic feet of water into the ocean every second, through a channel ten miles wide and thirteen hundred feet in depth—the stream whose strong fresh current, strewn with floating islands, reeds, and timber torn from the shores of the great lakes and giant forests of the interior, had first been noticed by Diego Cam when still out of sight of land four hundred years before—was the same that they had seen pent up between narrow

walls of rock, and bounding over boulder and ledge.
In the journey of seven thousand two hundred miles,
one hundred and fourteen members of the original
party had perished. Many had fallen in battle or by
treachery; still more were the victims of African
diseases. Some the " gulfs had washed down;" but
a goodly remnant survived all danger and reached
the " Happy Isles"—either those that own the sway
of Seyd Burghash of Zanzibar, or the still more fortunate lands ruled over by Her Gracious Majesty.

CHAPTER IV.

THE WATER-PARTING OF THE CONGO.

HE feat of crossing Africa from ocean to ocean was not first performed by Stanley. Commander Cameron had, two years previously, travelled from the east to the west coast; and twenty years had elapsed since Dr. Livingstone had walked from Kuruman, his mission station in the Kalihari Desert, northwestwards to the Atlantic at St. Paul de Loanda, and then retraced his steps eastwards to the other side of the continent at the Zambesi mouth. But early in the century the native traders Pedro Joas Baptista and Anastacio José, known as the " Pombeiros," had proceeded from the colony of Angola to Teté, on the Zambesi, in the Mozambique possessions of Portugal. Since Stanley's day Major Serpa Pinto has crossed Africa transversely from Loanda to Natal. Livingstone, Cameron, Pinto, and the Pombeiros all traversed the water-shed separating the Congo from the basin of the Zambesi; and so, while

we are still absolutely ignorant of the region that
supplies the water which the Lualaba draws from the
north of the Equator, we do know something of the
southern reservoirs from whence comes the other half
of its store.

It is a sloppy country, this region of the " water-
partings," even in the dry season ; during the rains it
is a vast quagmire. The stupendous rock and cataract
scenery of the main stream of the Congo we will seldom
meet with here : but it has natural marvels of its
own that are worthy of notice. Brilliant battle-pieces
can no longer be woven into the narrative ; for, unlike
the impetuous American, Livingstone and Cameron,
when they found the path barred by force, sat down
and sought to weary out the enemy by patience, or
turned aside or turned back rather than meet violence with violence. Even cannibals get scarce ; yet
on this route we will meet some examples of sheer
brute barbarity and truculent ruffianism that will not
easily be paralleled even in Africa.

Cameron crossed to the left bank of the Lualaba
at Nyangwe, and struck south-westwards, because he
did not choose to fight with the natives for a passage
down the stream, even if he had had the prospect of
doing so with success. He hoped, and he made many
endeavours, to return to the Lualaba ; but he was
baffled in every attempt by the unrelenting opposition of the aborigines. So his route bended more
and more to the south, towards the sources of the
river, and at last he abandoned all idea of regaining
the main stream ; " recognizing it to be my duty," he

says, "not to risk a single life unnecessarily, and
feeling that the merit of any geographical discovery
would be irretrievably marred by shedding a single
drop of native blood."

But despite this resolve, the march was by no
means without warlike incident. On one occasion,
tramping up the banks of the Lomane river, the
traveller's cogitations were disagreeably interrupted
by a flight of arrows rustling about him. One of the
arrows glanced off his shoulder, and getting a peep
of the bowman dodging behind a tree, Cameron flung
down his rifle and started off in pursuit. Catching
up his adversary after a brisk chase, the gallant
naval officer administered to him a well-earned
drubbing with his fists, smashed his bow and arrows,
and dismissed him with a "stern admonition" that pro-
jected the savage a yard or two into the forest. This
specimen of British retaliation had an impressive
effect on the other natives who were looking on
from their lurking-places in the bushes, and they
were soon swearing friendship and performing
dances in the stranger's honour. Only a few marches
further on, however, the party fell into another
ambuscade, and arrows and spears began to whistle
around. The savages followed them on both sides of
the track, keeping out of range of guns in the open,
but creeping up and shooting at the travellers where-
ever there was cover of jungle or grass. "The whit!
whit! of the long arrows through the trees created a
very unpleasant sensation," we are told; but so long
as none of the exploring party were wounded, the

A WEIR BRIDGE.

Page 193

leader " kept on never minding." By-and-by, a
village was observed in the jungle ahead, and tired
of being made marks of, the members of the expedition made a rush for it, while the inhabitants cleared
out at the other end; and here Cameron fortified himself, and so stoutly repelled all attempts to capture his
position that the villagers were fain to agree to a par-
ley and allow the travellers to go their way in peace.

The route from the Lualaba to the Lomane, and
southwards along the banks of the latter stream, leads
through a great plain covered with forest and scrub,
and cut up at short intervals by innumerable water-
courses. In and out of these gulches the path continually dips and rises, except at places where the
natives of the country have thrown across a "sus-
pension bridge" for their convenience, composed of
stout cables of ratan fastened to the trunks of the
trees on each side of the stream, with guy ropes and
wattled balustrade made of smaller creepers, and cut
lengths of bamboo forming the roadway. Other
ingeniously constructed bridges there are in this
country which are designed to serve a double use.
These are " fish-weirs," formed of long poles, forty feet
or more in length, driven into the bed of the stream,
crossing each other in the shape of a " St. Andrew's
cross," and joined together by other poles laid hori-
zontally along the line of junction. In the water
below, the nets of the fishermen are spread between
the lower ends of the poles, while the wayfarer can
march dry-shod from bank to bank along the
V-shaped space between their tops.

Over these precarious structures, and with many
ups and downs, the party continued their way, till
they came to Kilemba, the head-town of Kasongo,
the king of the great country of Rua or Urua.
Kasongo—which is this precious potentate's title, not
his name—is perhaps, on the whole, the most ogrish
person to be met with in the interior of Africa. His
land is an extensive one, stretching from the margin
of the Tanganyika to the water-shed of the Congo with
the Zambesi : and he firmly believes that he is the
most powerful monarch on the face of the earth, the
only individual worthy of being spoken of in the
same breath with him being his relative and neighbour, Muata Yanvo, great chief of Ulunda, which
immediately adjoins Rua to the west. Like other
ogres whom we read of in story, Kasongo was not in his
den when the travellers arrived. He was abroad on
his usual pursuit of plundering and slaughtering in
a distant corner of his domain ; and his chief wife
had to do the honours of the Kilemba court till his
return. This did not happen for four months ; and
after his arrival, a period as long elapsed before the
expedition was allowed to proceed. Cameron had,
therefore, excellent opportunities of studying the
" noble savage " close at hand and at his leisure. In
one respect, at least, Kasongo is above European
sovereigns, for none have claimed such absolute
power. The lives, persons, and property of his subjects are at his disposal, to use or abuse as he will ;
and generally his will is a very cruel and rapacious
one. Something of the nature of chiefship in Rua

may be gathered from the ceremonies attending the burial of the monarch :—

"The first proceeding is to divert the course of a stream, and in its bed to dig an enormous pit, the bottom of which is covered with living women. At one end a woman is placed on her hands and knees, and upon her back the dead chief, covered with his beads and other treasures, is seated, being supported on either side by one of his wives, while his second wife sits at his feet. The earth is then shovelled in on them, and all the women are buried alive, except the second wife, to whom custom grants the privilege of being killed before the huge grave is filled in. This being completed, a number of male slaves— sometimes forty or fifty—are slaughtered, and their blood poured upon the grave ; after which, the river is allowed to resume its course."

When a "small chief" dies, " two or three wives and a few slaves only " are sacrificed ; but on the occasion of the funeral obsequies of so great a man as the late Kasongo, it is said that no fewer than a hundred women were buried alive ! Such hideous barbarities would be looked upon as incredible, and the story as a monstrous libel on human nature, were the evidence not so undoubted. Kasongo's household furniture consists of his relatives and the members of his harem. When it is his royal pleasure to sit down, one of his wives has to "make a back" for him. When he walks about his house, he must have a carpet of living human bodies on which to tread ; and when he stretches himself to sleep, his mattress must be composed of a pile of his fellow-creatures. The first thing that Cameron observed on being ushered into the presence of this wretched creature, was the mutilation to which his courtiers and retainers had been almost universally subjected. Ears, noses, and lips were cropped off on the most trifling provocation, or out of simple caprice; and Kasongo's prime favourite showed the tokens of his master's favour in his wanting not only the features mentioned, but also his hands.

During the traveller's stay with him, the king was generally drunk and half mad with pombe and bhang; and his filthy, debauched, and brutal face was no more pleasant to look at than his doings are agreeable to dwell on. Yet there were some, calling themselves Europeans, dwelling at Kasongo's court, that found his company and ways very much to their liking. These were the Portuguese half-breeds, in whose hands is the slave-trade, which is conducted on a large scale between this part of the interior and the west coast. At Kasongo's we part company with the Moslem slave-trader; but we are introduced to a still more truculent scoundrel—the Christian kidnapper from the Portuguese settlements, who is as much more vile than the Arab as the civilization from which he has degenerated is higher than that of Mohammedan Africa. In fact, one feels some compunction of feeling towards the Arab pioneers from the east coast when about to see the last of them for some time. Among them are what may be called honourable men, according to their dim lights. Several of these adventurous merchants in black and white ivory were very helpful and kindly towards Livingstone, and Stanley also struck up a friendship with members of the fraternity. No one could have given more proofs of generous friendship than were shown towards Cameron at Kasongo's by Jumah Mericani, "a fine, portly Arab, with a dash of the tar-brush:" and he and others were ready to admit that if they could find any more reputable business they would be glad to abandon slaving.

No such scruples seem ever to have visited the Portuguese half-breed slave-traders. If there is a white sheep in that exceedingly dingy flock, he has escaped the notice of a series of very keen-eyed observers. The representatives of West Coast civilization at Kasongo's, Jose Antonio Alvez and Lourenço da Souza Coimbra, were bad specimens even of their class. Alvez was an ugly old black, scarcely to be distinguished in hue and features from a full-blooded negro, who had industriously added to his natural bad qualities those acquired by a lifetime of slave-hunting and murder. Coimbra was a younger but perhaps more unmitigated ruffian. These were the companions with whom, and their slave-gang, the English explorer had to make his journey to the Portuguese colony.

But, first, he made two interesting trips to lakes in the neighbourhood of Kasongo's capital. One was to the neighbourhood of Lake Kassali, some days' march to the south-eastward, and on the central channel of the Lualaba drainage—the river Luapula, which

Livingstone saw bursting out of Lake Moero, after passing through Lake Bangweolo, being, according to Cameron's information, only a western branch of the main stream, which it joins at Lake Kamolondo. The Kassali Lake, which is of considerable size, must be an interesting place in more ways than one. The true Lualaba and a great tributary, the Lufira, pour themselves into it: and the united waters, escaping from its northern end, form a series of lake-like expansions as they slowly drain towards Kamolondo. On the lake itself are floating islands, inhabited by numerous populations of fishermen. The matted growths of aquatic plants fringing its shores are cut off in sections, and towed to the centre of the lake. Logs, brushwood, and earth are laid on the floating platform, until it acquires a consistency capable of supporting a native hut and a plot of bananas and other fruit trees, with a small flock of goats and poultry. The island is anchored by a stake driven into the bed of the lake; and if the fishing become scarce, or should other occasion occur for shifting his domicile, the proprietor simply draws the peg, and shifts his little floating mansion, farm, and stock whither he chooses.

Mr. Cameron was not so lucky as to be able to examine these curious habitations; in fact, he was only able to get a look of the lake from the highlands above it. The lake-dwellers having consulted a wizard, or " medicine-man "—who is almost as important a member of African society as the king— and this personage having produced his "fetiches" and

charms, and drummed and postured to his heart's
content, announced as the result of his hocus-pocus,
that if the white man were allowed to approach
nearer to the lake, its waters would dry up! The
traveller had, therefore, reluctantly to turn back.

What he heard concerning the country beyond was
fitted to stimulate his curiosity and ours. He was
told, for instance, of a river which produced leprosy
in any one drinking its waters; and of a tree of so
deadly a shade, that of a trading party who lay down
to rest under its branches, nothing was found next
morning save their skeletons and the ivory they carried. More wonderful still was a district where the
villagers were on excellent speaking and visiting terms
with the lions of the neighbourhood. As many as
two hundred of the friendly animals would sometimes attend the village gatherings, and walk affably
about among their hosts, who would regale their
four-legged guests with honey, goats, and sheep; and
when a lion of their acquaintance died, they would
mourn for him as for a relative. Away towards the
head-waters of the Lualaba and Lufira are situated
the Katanga copper-workings, which supply brace-
lets, necklaces, anklets, and other ornaments in brass
to a large portion of Central Africa; and here, it
is said, gold is found in quantity, but is flung aside
as "soft" and useless. Considering the close neighbourhood of these workings to districts visited by
European traders, this is, perhaps, the most incredible
story of all. Much more definite and authentic were
the particulars gathered concerning the underground

villages on the Lufira. The ramifications of these extend right across the bed of the stream; and the subterranean chambers are said to be lofty and spacious, with roofs supported by pillars of white marble and quartz, formed of the unhewn rock. They have many passages of exit and entrance, so that if their enemies follow them into their retreat, they may find themselves attacked in rear by the cave-dwellers who have escaped by another door.

All these contrivances for defence and hiding show how insecure is human life in a region where every petty chief's hand is against his neighbour, and where the king is the curse and terror of his people. The huts in the vicinity of Kasongo's capital are buried deep in the jungle, and thickly fenced round with thorns, the only approach being by a long, low, narrow passage, through which one often has to crawl on hands and knees, and which can be closed by a portcullis-like contrivance composed of bars of wood. Another illustration of the universal state of fear in which the inhabitants live is seen in the lake-villages of Lake Mohrya, on the right of Cameron's route, to which he made an excursion. Three such villages are built on the waters of the shallow lake, and detached huts are sprinkled over its surface. The houses are built on piles, six feet above the level of the water. Underneath nets are hung, and the canoe is moored in which the inhabitants of this African Venice make trips to their cultivated fields on the shore to fetch away their produce of grain and fruit. Ordinary morning calls between the lake-

dwellers are paid by simply swimming from hut
to hut. So timid are these people that Cameron
could open no communication with them, and those
whom he surprised among their crops rushed at the
top of their speed to their canoes, and paddled out
into the lake.

Considering the experiences of the people of these
countries, no one can feel surprised at the suspicion
and hostility they show towards strangers. Terrible
evidence of their wrongs was seen by Cameron on
his journey along with Alvez and Coimbra from
King Kasongo's to the Portuguese territory. Where
these swaggering bravoes felt themselves to be masters,
they hectored and bullied to their heart's content,
rummaged and plundered the fields and villages from
which the inhabitants had fled in terror, and destroyed
what they could not carry away. But when they
came to a village where the population were armed
with guns, and were prepared to use them, the heroes
put on a meek and lamb-like demeanour, and made
obsequious proffers of presents of cloth and beads.
After one short absence, Coimbra appeared in camp
with a gang of fifty-two female slaves, the produce
of the sack and destruction of at least ten villages,
each having a population of from one hundred to two
hundred souls. These poor creatures were loaded
with their children and the plunder of their own
homes, and covered with weals and sores ; and so
mercilessly cruel was their treatment, that Cameron
felt an almost uncontrollable impulse to cut them
free, and to seize their brutal captor by the scruff

of the neck and shake his wretched soul out of him.

The march began in the end of June 1875, nine months after Cameron's arrival at Kasongo's. It led first through Ussambi, between the head-streams of the Lualaba and the Lomame, over wooded hills, flat-topped table-lands of sandstone, and numerous rivers with banks fringed with marshes—a beautiful and diversified but difficult country. Then it entered Ulunda, the realm of Muata Yanvo. The travellers gave a wide berth to the chief town of that great man, who in character and pursuits was another edition of Kasongo. The last white man that visited him had never returned. Besides, there had been a revolution at court. Muata Yanvo had been trying to add to the list of his accomplishments by practising "vivi-section" on some of his wives, and the others, taking fright, had joined in a conspiracy against him, and the despot of Ulunda was a fugitive. The country lies in a long strip on both banks of the Kassabe River—probably the same as Stanley's Ikelemba. Where Cameron crossed Ulunda, near its southern end, it is a thickly-wooded undulating land, full of countless streams flowing towards the Congo, and inhabited by a wild repulsive-looking people. The hollows between the undulations are occupied by "sponges"—the saturated marshes overgrown with water-plants, with which Livingstone made so fatal acquaintance near Bangweolo.

When the frontier of Ulunda is passed—the road still leading south-westwards—we reach Lovale, a still more swampy country, lying across the water-shed of the Congo and the Zambesi. The sources of the two rivers are interlocked or dovetailed into each other; and at intervals of two or three miles streams flowing towards the Atlantic and towards the Indian Ocean are crossed alternately. These great plains are comparatively dry during the heats of summer, but in the season of the rains they are vast quagmires covered waist-deep with water, and a large lake unites the two great river-systems. By cutting a canal about twenty miles in length through this level country, with light portages for passing the rapids on the river courses, internal navigation might, says Cameron, be established between the east and west coast; and this may be one of the great works for the development of Central Africa which the future will see accomplished.

West of Lovale is Kibokwe, where swamp again gives place to almost uninterrupted forest, and we begin to ascend the slope towards the high coast ranges that form the western edge of the great table-land of Central Africa. The eastern scarp of the tableau we crossed, it will be remembered, soon after leaving Zanzibar; and the water-shed between the Congo and the Zambesi seems to be a low ridge, transversely connecting these two mountain walls. The rearing of bees is the chief occupation of the people of Kibokwe, and they are also clever workers in iron. Still further westwards is the country of Bihé, on the upper basin of the river Kwanza, which flows into the Atlantic to the south of the Congo. Bihé, a region of rocks and hills and running streams, is the border-land between savagery and civilization; and its chief town is the great mart for the exchange of tropical produce—chiefly bees'-wax, ivory, palm-oil, india-rubber, cinnabar, and slaves—for the old rifles, glass beads, and brass wire which the white traders bring up from the coast.

Beyond Bihé a still more beautiful highland country is reached. No human pen or pencil, Cameron says, could do justice to the loveliness and grandeur of the scenery of Bailunda, a land of "rocky hills, with brawling burns rushing along their rugged courses, with here and there falls from twenty to thirty feet in height, the crystal water sparkling in the sunset as it dashes from crag to crag. Large tree-ferns grow on the banks, and among the bushes are myrtle, jasmine, and other flowering shrubs; while beautiful ferns, similar to maiden-hair and other delicate kinds, flourish in the damp crevices of the rocks In the foreground are glades in the woodland, varied by knolls crowned by groves of large English-looking trees, sheltering villages with yellow, thatched roofs; plantations with the fresh green of young crops and bright red of newly-hoed ground in vivid contrast; whilst in the far distance are mountains of endless and pleasing variety of form, gradually fading away until they blend with the blue of the sky. White fleecy clouds drift overhead; and the hum of bees, the bleating of goats and crowing of cocks, break the stillness of the air."

With this glimpse of it in its fairest aspect, we pass from the charmed circle of Central Africa; for soon the summit of the range is reached, and the steep slope to the coast begins, first through heavy forests of palm, with rank thickets of creepers, then down the lower foot-hills, thinly sprinkled over with baobabs, euphorbias, and cactuses, and other thorny growths, the unfailing signs of a droughty climate, until at length we are on the arid strip along the sea-shore, among the well-known, thick-lipped, flat-nosed negro peoples of the west coast, and by the familiar waves of the Atlantic.

Part Third.—The Zambesi.

CHAPTER I.

FROM LAKE DILOLO TO LAKE NGAMI.

> " Away, away from the dwellings of men !
> By the wild deer's haunt and the buffalo's glen ;
> By valleys remote where the oribi plays,
> Where the gnu, the gazelle, and the hartebeest graze ;
> And the gemsbok and eland unhunted recline
> By the skirts of gray forest o'erhung with wild vine ;
> And the elephant browses at peace in his wood ;
> And the river-horse gambols unscared in the flood ;
> And the mighty rhinoceros wallows at will
> In the Vley, where the wild ass is drinking his fill."
> PRINGLE.

LAKE DILOLO is the connecting link between the Congo and the Zambesi. It is not much of a lake—a mere pond, in fact, compared with the great inland seas we have lately been making acquaintance with. It is triangular in shape, and some eight miles in length by three miles in breadth at the widest end. It is more worthy of curious notice, however, than many lakes that far exceed it in extent. It puzzled Livingstone on a first view; but by an

attentive consideration of it he was first enabled to
grasp firmly a clue to the physical configuration of
South Central Africa. When the doctor first saw
its waters—on that famous journey of his in 1852-4
from the Cape of Good Hope to the capital of the
Portuguese possessions on the west coast—he found
a broad, still channel draining out of Lake Dilolo
towards the Zambesi. A few months after, he again
approached its shores, this time from the northern
side ; for he was on his way back across the continent, in fulfilment of his pledge to restore his Makololo guides and companions to their homes. He was
surprised to observe that another slow-flowing, rush-
choked stream, a mile in breadth, escaped from the
other extremity of the lake, and poured down the slope
towards the Congo. On both occasions Livingstone
was ill with the fever and ague that are the constant companions of the traveller in these damp, flat
regions ; and on his north-westward march he had
been two days without food when he sighted
Dilolo. He was able, however, to conquer the
disease sufficiently to satisfy himself that this little
lake, situated four thousand seven hundred feet
above the sea-level, is placed exactly on the water-
shed between the Atlantic and the Indian Ocean,
and distributes the contents of its basin in impartial
share between the two seas. A drop of rain, as it
is blown by the wind to the one or the other end of
Dilolo, may reinforce the vast tumbling flood that
roars through the gorges of the Congo, and rushes
out for sixty miles into the salt waters of the

Atlantic, or may make with the Zambesi the
dizzy leap over the great Victoria Falls, and mingle
with the eastern ocean. No well authenticated case
of an exactly similar phenomenon is known. Lake
Kivo may form the corresponding bond of union
between the Congo and the Nile, but regarding it
we have only hearsay evidence. There is the well-
known instance of the "two-ocean fountain" in the
Rocky Mountains, the stream from which, split in
two by some trifling obstacle in the path, contributes
half of its waters to the stormy Atlantic, while the
other half finds a resting-place in the Pacific. Hum-
boldt has described the curious phenomenon of the
Cassiquiare river in Venezuela, that "flows in two
directions"—towards the Rio Negro and the great
estuary of the Amazon, and towards the Orinoco and
the Caribbean Sea; and further on we will meet
with something closely resembling the Cassiquiare,
uniting the Zambesi with Lake Ngami. But no
well authenticated case of a lake with exactly similar position and functions as Dilolo is known to
geography.

Apart from the eccentric double part it plays, the
features of Dilolo are tame and ordinary enough. It
has, of course, its hippopotami and its crocodiles—every
water in Central Africa has; and almost equally, of
course, it is fringed with inundated marshes covered
with a profuse growth of mat-rushes, cane, papyrus,
lotus, and arum. Round it stretch wide plains,
limitless apparently as the sea, on which, for many
months of the year, the stagnant water rests, bal-

ancing itself, as it were, between the two sides of
the continent, and unable to make up its mind
whether to favour the east coast or the west with its
tribute. Only at hollow spots here and there can
the presence of the water be detected by the eye
that glances over these immense flats. They are
overgrown with tall grass with stalks sometimes an
inch and a half in diameter, through which it is
terribly tough work to force a passage. Most people
would consider the fact of the surface being covered
with a foot or two of water an addition to their misfortunes; but Livingstone had a knack of extracting
comfort from his very troubles, and descants sometimes on the "refreshing" feel of the moisture about
his feet. In the rainy season this drowned vegetation has a sere and yellow look. No trees break the
horizon, the little islands in the fen bearing only a
low growth of scrub, and the landscape is dismal and
monotonous in the extreme. Dilolo itself means
"despair," and the dwellers near it tell a melancholy
story, curiously resembling the tale of the Cities of
the Plain, and the traditions handed down regarding
some of the lakes in Central Asia, of how a venerable wanderer came to this spot one evening, and
begged for the charity of shelter and food; how the
churlish inhabitants mocked his petition, with the
exception of one poor man, who gave the stranger a
nook by his fire and the best his hut afforded; and
how, after a terrible night of tempest and lightning,
the hospitable villager found his guest gone, and the
site of his neighbours' dwellings occupied by a lake.

When the rains have ceased, and the hot sun has begun to dry up the moisture, the outlook is more cheerful, and Livingstone describes the beautiful effects produced by a small flower that carpets these plains. A broad golden band stretches across the path, composed of flowers of every shade of yellow, from palest lemon to deepest orange; then succeeds a strip of blue, varying from the lightest tint to purple; and so band follows band, with the regularity and uniformity of the stripes on a zebra's hide. Another little flower, whose leaves are furnished with hairs on the tip of each of which a drop of dew sparkles in the mornings, adds another charm to this strange parti-coloured country.

The explorer is glad, however, to escape from these spongy water-sheds—which, with their springs spouting water in all directions, have been compared by Livingstone to the "rose" of a watering-pan or water-cart—and to pass down into the shades of the forests of the Zambesi, where at least there will be a change of discomforts and a variety of scenery. In traversing the region from the Cape four modes of conveyance were tested by the missionary. There is first the bullock waggon, familiar in the English colony, an admirably convenient and pleasant method in the dry open plains to the southward, but not practicable in the reedy wildernesses adjoining the Zambesi. Riding on bullock-back was also a mode of travelling which Livingstone had frequently to resort to from sheer inability to walk from weakness. Of course marching on foot is the best of all plans when a thorough and minute acquaintance with the district traversed is desired. But the disadvantages of it are obvious, and for easy and rapid progress there is nothing like "paddling your own canoe," or better still, having it paddled for you by skilled boatmen, down the deep reaches and over the rushing shallows of the third of the great African rivers. Before the main stream of the Zambesi is reached the silvan shades of the Lotembwa and the Leeba have to be threaded—dark moss-coloured rivers flowing between dripping banks of evergreen forest and jungle, with frequent clearings, where the villagers raise their crops of manioc, the plant that yields the tapioca of commerce, and that here, as in Angola, furnishes the chief food of the inhabitants.

Fetich worship flourishes in these damp and gloomy woods. In their depths a fantastically carved demon-face, staring from a tree, will often startle the intruder in the spirit haunts; or a grotesque representation of a lion, or a crocodile, or of the "human face divine," made of rushes plastered over with clay, and with shells or beads for eyes, will be found perched in a seat of honour, with offerings of food and ornaments laid on the rude altar. Whether human sacrifices are offered at these shrines, as is said to be the case in parts of Muata Yanvo's and Kasongo's territories, cannot positively be said. But the most simple and trifling acts are "taboo;" and unless the traveller is exceedingly wary in all that he does or says—in his rising up and his sitting down, in where he lays his rifle and how or when he eats or drinks—he is likely mulcted in heavy fines, or looked upon as a doomed and accursed man, who will bring misfortune on all who aid or approach him. The "medicine-man" has a terrible power, which he often exercises, over the lives and property of his fellows; and a denunciation of "witch-craft" is generally equivalent to a sentence of death. Here, as elsewhere in Central Africa, the ordeal of "muava," or poison-drinking, is the method left open to the victim to escape from a charge of this kind. If his stomach should reject the decoction, he is considered innocent; while the more likely probability of his death is held to establish his guilt. After all, we should remember that in these and other superstitions, such as the evil eye, the poor Balovale are only a few generations behind our own enlightened land.

A great source of the witch-finders' revenue is "weather-making;" but, unlike the prophets in the arid deserts to the south, the magicians of this moist and cloudy region devote their energies to keeping off the rain and not to bringing it down from heaven. Of course, if they persevere long enough the rain ceases to fall. The credulous Balovale believe implicitly that this has been produced by the "medicine" they have purchased so dearly, just as the Bechuana place entire trust in the ability of their rain-makers, when handsomely hired, to bring showers down on the thirsty ground by virtue of drumming and capering.

The behaviour of the inhabitants of these remote villages on the sudden apparition among them of a white man is apt to shake the latter's complacent notion that the superior good looks of his own race are universally acknowledged. Their standard of beauty is quite different from ours. Sometimes it is fat that is chiefly sought after, and the desirableness of a wife is measured by the number of pounds she weighs. Sometimes it is intense sootiness of hue that is supposed to lend the principal charm to complexion, though the chief races of the Zambesi —for instance, the Makololo—are by no means quite black, but rather of a dark coffee colour. Often it is a peculiarity of ornamentation or tattooing, a special style of head-dress, or some preposterous disfigurement of the nose, lips, or ears, on which the female population mainly rely for making themselves attractive. The wearing of clothes is regarded as a practice fairly provocative of laughter, and as "improper" as the want of them would be in Europe. As for the long hair of the stranger and his shaggy beard and whiskers like the mane of a lion, nothing, according to their notions, could be more hideous, and examination alone will convince them that he is not wearing a wig over his natural locks of crisp wool. Possessing these ideas, the white man—especially if he have blue eyes and red whiskers—is in their eyes a frightful hobgoblin, before whom the village girls run away screaming with terror, and the children hide trembling behind their mothers, much as would happen if a naked black monster, with green hair and yellow eyes, were suddenly to appear in the street of one of our own little country hamlets.

In spite of the most minute explanations, it is impossible to eradicate from these poor negro people's minds the idea that there is something supernatural about the white man, with his wonderful knowledge, his mysterious apparatuses, and his magical coming from and departure to the sea; and they insist on regarding us as a race of mermen, who have the powers of light and darkness more completely at our command than even the most skilled of their medicine-men. At the village of Shinté, the principal chief on the Leeba river, and a vassal of Muata Yanvo, Livingstone was very kindly treated by the great man, who received him seated in state under the shade of a banian tree, with his hundred wives seated behind him and his band of drummers and marimba-players performing in front; and out of gratitude the doctor treated the distinguished party to an entertainment with the magic-lantern. The subject was the death of Isaac, and the court looked on with awe as the gigantic figures, with flowing oriental robes, prominent noses, and ruddy complexions, appeared upon the curtain. But when Abraham's uplifted hand, armed with the dagger, was seen descending, the ladies of the court, fancying that it was about to be sheathed in their own bosoms instead of Isaac's, sprang to their feet, and with shouts of "Mother, mother!" rushed "helter-skelter, tumbling pell-mell over each other and over the little idol-houses and tobacco-bushes;" and it was impossible to bring one of them back to witness the patriarch's subsequent fortunes.

GAME ON THE ZAMBESI.

On the lower part of the Leeba the scenery becomes
very beautiful and richly diversified. The alterna-
tion of hill and dale, open glade and forest, past
which the canoe bears us swiftly, reminds one of a
carefully kept park. Animal life becomes more
plentiful with every mile of southing, and the broad
meadows bordering the stream are pastured by great
herds of wild animals—buffaloes, elands, antelopes, and
zebras, with an occasional elephant and rhinoceros—
which are so tame that they may be slaughtered in
scores before they begin to take alarm. Below the
confluence of the Leeba with the Leeambye, or main
branch of the Zambesi—which flows from the east
through a district that has never been explored—the
abundance of game on the banks of the river is even
more remarkable. The air, too, is often darkened by
the flight of innumerable water-fowl—scarlet ibises,
fish-hawks, cranes, and waders and divers of many
varieties for which names have not yet been in-
vented—the earth teems with insect life, and the
water swarms with fish.

As an instance of the prodigious quantity and
exceeding tameness of the wild animals here, Livingstone mentions that "eighty-one buffaloes defiled
in slow procession before our fire one evening
within gunshot, and herds of splendid elands stood
by day without fear at two hundred yards' distance;" while all through the night the lions
were heard roaring close to the camp. In the
heat of the day the sleek elands, tall as ordinary
horses, with bulky, ox-like bodies and delicately

striped skins, browse or recline under the shade of the clumps of forest; troops of graceful, agile, fleet-footed antelopes of smaller species scour across the pasture-lands to seek the cool retreat of some deep dell in the woods; or a solitary rhinoceros comes grunting down to the bank in search of some soft place where he can roll his horny hide in the mud. The trees themselves have a variety and beauty which the sombre evergreen foliage higher up lacks, and which is equally wanting in the thorny, dust-coloured growths of the desert further south. The banian, or Indian fig, is a stately and prominent feature in the landscape, and its habit of sending down branches that take root and shoot up again in a new growth, until a single plant forms a grove of itself, has suggested the native name, meaning "the tree that walks." The lofty stem and graceful top of the palmyra palm often shows itself above the other forest vegetation: the pandanus, draped from its topmost sword-shaped leaf to its exposed roots in lovely mosses, lichens, and orchids, is always a beautiful object; and the huts of the natives peep out from bowers of bananas, broad-fronded plantains, and flowering hibiscus.

The voyage down-stream is by no means without incident. The river swarms with hippopotami and crocodiles. The former lead a lazy, sleepy life by day in the bottom of the stream, coming now and then to the surface to breathe, and exchange a snort of recognition with their acquaintances, and are only too well pleased to let the passer-by go in peace, if he will only leave them alone. In districts where they are hunted they are wary, and take care to push no more than the tip of their snouts out of water in some bed of rushes, where they breathe so softly that they cannot be heard. But in a pool where they have not been disturbed, they can be seen swimming and "blowing off steam" freely, the female hippopotamus having frequently the squat little figure of her calf riding on her neck. Certain elderly behemoths who are expelled the herd become soured in temper, and are dangerous to encounter; and so also is a mother who has been robbed of her young. Such a one made an attack on Livingstone's boat when descending the Zambesi in 1855, and butting it from beneath, tilted the fore end out of water, and flung one of the rowers into the stream. By diving and holding on to the grass at the bottom, while the angry beast was looking for him on the surface, he escaped its vengeance; and the boat being fortunately close to the shore the rest of the crew also got off unscathed.

The alligators on this part of the Zambesi are peculiarly rapacious and aggressive, and the chances are that anybody unlucky enough to fall into the river will find his way into the maw of a watchful crocodile. Every year these ferocious reptiles carry off hundreds of human victims, chiefly women while filling their water-jars, or men whose canoes are accidentally upset; and the inhabitants in their turn make a prey of the saurian, being extremely fond both of its flesh and eggs. The crocodile prefers surprises to open methods of attack. He skulks behind a bank of rushes, or lies in wait at the bottom of a pool, and rushes out as soon as he sees a human limb in the water. Sometimes, however, when "sharp set" with hunger, and where a favourable opportunity occurs, he will haul his body ashore, and waddle boldly up the bank on his stumpy legs to the attack; or if, while disporting himself on shore, his wicked green eyes fall on some likely victim in the stream, he has been known to scuttle with great alacrity through the rushes, and, plunging into the river, make openly and open-jawed for his prey. The young show their vicious temper almost as soon as they are out of the shell; and one savage little wretch, some two feet long, made a snap at Dr. Livingstone's legs while walking along the side of a stream in the Zambesi region, that made the explorer jump aside with more agility than dignity.

Some distance below the junction of the Leeba the Zambesi enters the Barotse Valley. This is one of the most fertile and most unhealthy districts in the interior of Africa. It is a land flowing with milk and honey. It is stocked with great herds of domestic cattle — which are of two varieties, one high standing, with enormous horns nearly nine feet between the tips, and a beautifully formed little white breed—and roamed over by wild game of every kind in immense numbers. It could grow grain enough to support ten times the inhabitants it at present contains; but the resident here, if he survive the process of acclimatization, must lay his account for periodical ague, rheumatism, and fever. Like the lower valley of the Nile, the Barotse country is

every year inundated over its whole surface by the
waters of the river, which deposit a layer of fertilizing slime on its surface. The banks of the Zambesi,
for some distance above and below this district, are
high and cliffy, presenting reach after reach of fine
rock and woodland scenery, while the stream runs
swiftly over a stony bed. For a hundred miles in
the Barotse Valley the stream has a deep and winding course, and the hills withdraw to a distance of
fifteen miles from either bank. To the foot of these
hills the waters extend in flood time, and the valley
becomes temporarily one of the "Lake Regions" of
Central Africa, with the native villages, each built on
its artificial mound, showing above the flood as islands.

At the lower end of the valley the rocky spurs
again approach each other, and the river forces its
way through a narrow defile, in which, in flood time,
the water rises to a height of sixty feet above its
ordinary level. Here are situated the Gonye Falls,
which are a serious impediment to the navigation of
the Upper Zambesi. But there is no such difficulty
or danger here for canoes ascending or descending as
poor Stanley met with on the Congo. Practice has
made the natives living near the falls adepts in the
work of transporting these craft over the rocky
ground; and as soon as a boat approaches the rapids
from above or below, it is slung on a pole and whisked
without delay by a party of sturdy porters to the
calmer water beyond. Below Gonye the water
bounds and rolls and bounces from bank to bank
and chafes over boulders in an alarming manner,

its breadth being contracted to a few hundred yards; but these swollen rapids might all be ascended, Livingstone thinks, when the river is full. After many leagues of these mad gambollings the Zambesi settles down again for a hundred miles of sober flow, and opens out into a magnificent navigable river, a mile or two from bank to bank.

Still more grand, however, are its dimensions after it receives a great, deep, dark-coloured, slow-flowing river—the Chobe—which enters it from the right, near where the Zambesi, which has been bending round from south to south-east, turns almost directly eastwards towards the Indian Ocean. The Chobe discharges by several mouths, through winding channels fringed with impenetrable beds of papyrus which assume the size of small palms. The stems are plaited and woven together into an almost solid mass by climbing convolvuluses with stalks as tough as whipcord, and by grasses with keen, sharp, serrated edges that cut like razors. Even the hippopotamus has no little ado in forcing a way through this reedy forest, and less weighty personages have to walk humbly in his track. So wide is the Zambesi below the entrance of the Chobe, that even a practised native eye cannot tell from the bank whether the land dimly seen beyond is island or the opposite shore; and the stream flows placidly and prosperously past, with no sign that it is almost within sight of a tremendous downfall.

But the fortunes of the main river must be left in the meantime, while we look a little up the Chobe.

It takes its rise in many springs and marshes to the south-west of Dilolo, and gathers in water from every quarter, which it squanders as freely again lower down its course. The only traveller who has crossed this line of country is Major Serpa Pinto, on his recent journey from Bihé to Natal. His descriptions may be coloured a little by the fervour of a Southern imagination; and perhaps we should accept with some slight reserve his accounts of marching for many days through morasses, with water up to his armpits, and only a handful of canary seed as food; of a species of antelope that lives under water like the hippopotamus, only coming now and then to the surface to breathe; and of a race of "white Africans," with Mongolian features, which some fanciful people have endeavoured to identify as a remnant of Genserie's Vandals who had fled all the way thither after the Arab conquest of Algiers. But there can be no doubt that Major Pinto made a most important and adventurous journey. He says that he found a spot where he could almost have placed his cap on the point of junction between streams draining towards the Atlantic, towards the Zambesi and the Indian Ocean, and towards the Kalihari Desert; and he tells of a river bed—the "Great Macaricari"—where the current flows in different directions at different periods of the year, so that when the Zambesi and its tributaries are in flood, the surplus water is poured off by the Macaricari to refresh the thirsty south, and when the level of the northern rivers fall, it restores to them a part of the water it had withdrawn.

The streams in these flat, damp regions, indeed, seem
to be all connected with each other by innumerable
creeks and arms, just as the stems of the trees are joined
together by the network of creepers. So the Chobe,
after having sent off several branches to the left to
reinforce the Zambesi, is supposed to depute another
body of water to the right to join a more southerly
river, the Embara. This stream, which rises on the
east side of the ranges behind Benguela, after receiving a tributary from the Chobe, splits into two. Its
more southerly branch, the Teoghe, finds its way into
Lake Ngami; and the more northerly, the Tzo, after
contributing unnecessarily to the overflowing cup
of the Chobe, turns also desertwards, and having
stretched an arm towards Ngami, passes on into the
waste, as the Zouga, with more halting step and
gradually failing power, until it is absorbed in the
great "salt-pans" of Kalihari.

As we have been moving southwards, a rapid and
wonderful change has come over the climate and the
vegetation. The damp, steaming atmosphere of the
marshes has given place to a dry and parching air
that drinks up every particle of moisture without
being satisfied. The dense, evergreen forests that shut
in the traveller, bounding his view like a wall on every
side, have been succeeded by wide, open, parched-up
downs, covered by sparse growths of dry euphorbia,
cactus, mimosa, and other gum-trees, with here and
there a vast baobab—giants eighty or a hundred feet
in girth, that may have been standing on these plains,
savants tell us, since the Great Deluge subsided. The

thickets bristle with thorny and leathery plants, and to force a way through them is a task compared with which crawling along a wall covered with broken glass would be a harmless and pleasant pastime. Some of these plants are armed with long spines that stab like daggers; others have sharp cutting edges that gash like knives; while a third class of them—such as the "wait-a-bit" thorn or "grapnel"—are furnished with a multitude of strong barbed hooks, ingeniously arranged so as to seize and hold the intruder in whatever direction he moves. Even the baobabs and gums gradually disappear, and with them all trace of running streams; for we have emerged on the other side of the region of the tropical rains and the great lakes, and are in the Kalihari Desert, the southern equivalent, though on a smaller scale, of the Great Sahara.

Lake Ngami and the wooded banks of the Zouga are the farthest outposts of the equatorial moisture towards the south, just as Lake Chad and the swamps of the White Nile mark its northern limits. Once, it is supposed—indeed the fact seems indubitable—the Zambesi and all its upper branches flowed down into this southern basin, and formed a goodly inland sea, until a great cataclysm happened that diverted the Zambesi waters to the east coast, leaving the central lake to dry up into the shallow Ngami, and the streams of these regions to wander about puzzled and uncertain whether to keep in the old tracks or follow in the new direction.

The discovery of Ngami was made on August 1,

1849, by Livingstone, in company with Oswell and Murray; and the circumstance marked an important era in the history of Central Africa. The sight of its wide stretch of unfailing water—or rather that of the forest-lined banks of the Zouga river that the travellers followed for some days previous to the discovery of the lake—demolished the theory of a burning desert occupying the interior of Africa from the Mediterranean to the Cape, and went far to prove. what has since been completely established, that "the fabulous torrid zone of parched and burning sand is a well-watered region resembling North America in its fresh-water lakes, and India in its hot, humid lowlands, jungles, ghauts, and cool highland plains."

Before the eyes of the travellers were gladdened by the sight of the waves breaking against the sandy or rush-fringed margin of the lake, they had been many times cheated into the belief that the goal of the journey had been reached. Once Oswell, walking ahead of the bullock-train, came suddenly in sight of a beautiful blue expanse on which the last rays of the setting sun were shining, and feeling sure this was "the lake" at last, he flung his cap into the air, and gave a shout that made his native companions imagine he had gone crazy. It was only one of the salt-pans, or *vleys*, so common in the Kalihari Desert, with a deceitful haze lying over the white incrustation. Some of these "pans" are of great extent—one of them, Ntwetwe, being a hundred miles in length; and the soil covered by the deposit of salt is, of course, useless for pasturage or any other purpose.

The Kalihari, however, is by no means an unmitigated desert; it is a fertile tract of country which happens to lack the grand requisite of a rainfall. The rain-laden winds from the east are robbed of their moisture in passing over the high ranges behind Natal and the Zulu and Kafir countries. Showers occasionally fall on the high grassy plains of the Transvaal table-land, and still more sparsely in the Bechuana country beyond; but with every mile westward the land becomes more dry and barren, and in the arid central and western regions rain is a phenomenon that may not occur for years. When a fall does take place, however, the transformation is almost miraculous. The surface soil is bound together by the roots of grasses and other plants that carpet the desert with luxuriant green so soon as they drink of the life-giving moisture. The most remarkable of the vegetable products of the Kalihari is the large water-melon with which, after a heavy rainfall, the ground will be covered for hundreds of square miles. Another plant shows only a small shoot above the surface, but by digging down a bulbous root full of moisture and as large as a child's head is found. Many species of plants, that have no such tendency under their natural conditions, suit themselves to circumstances in the Kalihari Desert by developing large bulbous underground protuberances in which to lay up a store of precious sap.

On the eastern verges of the Great Thirst Land this

waking to life out of the dust takes place periodically ; and nothing, says Livingstone, can exceed the beauty of the spring at Kolobeng, in the Bakwain country, west of the new British possession of the Transvaal. Immediately before the change the sun has been shining down on the hot " veldt" with a hotter glare than ever, and clouds of dust render outdoor existence almost unbearable. Then showers begin to fall; and when the ground has once been well soaked, a marvellous effect is produced. " In one day a tinge of green is apparent all over the landscape ; and in five or six days, the fresh leaves sprouting forth and the young leaves shooting up give an appearance of spring that it requires weeks of a colder climate to produce. The birds, which in the hot, dry, windy season had been silent, burst into merry, twittering songs, and are busy building their nests; and the earth teems with myriads of young insects," some of which, it may be noted, such as the white ant, are an important and favourite article of diet of the natives.

But the pride and glory of the Kalihari Desert are the herds of big and small game—giraffes, zebras, quaggas, gnus, ostriches, elands, hartebeestes, wild-beestes, gemsboks, klipspringers, gazelles, pokus, lech-wes, pallahs, and numerous other species of the deer and antelope tribe—that roam over its spacious plains. Great deeds of slaughter have been done with the rifle, and told over again in many a stirring book of African sport by Gordon Cumming, Andersson, and other mighty Nimrods, who were among the first of

the army of hunters who now annually invade these
bald solitudes in search of the trophies of hide, tusk,
and horn, which every year become more difficult to
obtain. The lion is practically the only "great cat"
whom the sportsman has to encounter, the tiger
being unknown in Africa, and the leopard comparatively rare. The "forest king" seems more at home
and comfortable in this tawny desert than in the
rank forests further north, probably because he finds
" food" more plentiful. Livingstone, in his usual contemptuous tone when speaking of this brute, describes
him as about as big as a donkey, and only brave at
roaring. Even the talk of his " majestic roar" he regards as " majestic twaddle ;" and he says he could
never tell the voice of the lion from the voice of the
ostrich, except from knowing that the quadruped
made a noise by night and the bird by day. The
lion would never dream of pitting himself against
the noble elephant, though he will tear a young elephant calf if he find one unprotected ; and he would
have still less chance in a contest with the armour-
cased rhinoceros. Even the buffalo is more than a
match for the "king of beasts ;" and Major Oswell
once came upon three lions who were having much
trouble in pulling a mortally wounded buffalo to the
ground.

Both the elephant and rhinoceros are hunted here
by the natives with packs of dogs. The yelping of
the curs at his heels completely "puts out" the
heavy-sided quarry, and while he is paying attention
to them, and making lumbering attempts to crush

them, the hunter creeps up and plants his bullet or poisoned arrow in a vital place. English sportsmen, however, disdaining such base aid, generally prefer to go out alone against the elephant, on foot or on horseback ; and in early days "bags" of as many as twenty would be made on a trip. The chase of the colossal animal, which attains his maximum height of twelve feet in the neighbourhood of the Limpopo, became in these circumstances really exciting and dangerous work ; for the African elephant, owing to the formation of his skull, cannot be brought down by a forehead shot like the Indian variety. Livingstone recommends to the intending hunter a course of preliminary practice at home for meeting an elephant's charge, by standing on a railway track until an express train is within a yard of him and then skipping aside.

The giraffe and ostrich are also hunted on horseback ; and the plan adopted with these gaunt, ungainly, but fleet-footed denizens of the waste is to press them at a hard gallop from the very first, which causes them to lose wind and sometimes to drop dead from excitement. The ostrich, when at the top of its speed, has been calculated to flee at the rate of some thirty miles an hour, so there is no hope of overtaking it in a long stern-chase ; but the stupid bird often delivers itself into the hands of its pursuers by running up-wind towards them—from an instinct of terror that it is being surrounded—instead of speeding straight ahead. Vast quantities of the desert game are killed in seasons of drought, when the torments of thirst drive them to the muddy springs and *vleys*, where their enemy man lies in wait for their lives ; and their numbers are said to be failing year by year, as civilization encroaches upon their haunts, and the spear and arrow are discarded for the gun.

The peoples of the Kalihari Desert are as characteristic of the soil and climate as its vegetable life and its four-footed beasts. There are two distinct races. The Ba-Kalihari are remnants of Bechuana tribes that have been driven into the desert by the pressure of stronger peoples behind. They are a pastoral or cattle-grazing folk, who cling under extraordinary difficulties to their ancestral love of the domestic animals, and may be seen laboriously watering their flocks of lean goats and meagre cattle by scooping up the precious fluid by the spoonful. A spindle-shanked, angular, pot-bellied, inoffensive people, they have to fight a hard battle for existence with Nature and with their neighbours. The Bushmen are true sons of the waste—wild men of the desert, who live by the chase and the foray. They are of diminutive stature ; and it has been suggested that, with the Akka and other pigmy tribes in the interior of the continent, they represent the real aborigines of Africa. Be that as it may, the real marvel about the Bushmen is how they contrive to exist at all in a region where water can only be obtained by sucking it up from the soil through reeds, and storing it in calabashes and ostrich shells against a time of still more grim drought. On the margin of the desert there are some thriving Bechuana communities, as for instance Shoshong, where the fine old chief, Khama, has protected the missionaries and traders, and taken the lead of his tribe, the Bamangwato, in adopting Christianity and civilized ways.

Another race, the Trek-Boers, or Emigrant Dutch farmers, have entered this region, fleeing from British rule in the Transvaal, as their fathers fled from the Cape Colony and Natal, and their vanguard, seeking a new Land of Promise, have unhitched their waggons on the shores of Lake Ngami.   As their coming always prognosticates troubles with the natives, and as gold-washers and diamond-diggers are thronging into the Kalihari Desert and Matabelé-land, we may expect to see British authority close to their heels, and perhaps at no very distant date established on the banks of the Zambesi.

CHAPTER II.

> " Calm he still pursued
> The stream that with a larger volume now
> Rolled through the labyrinthine vale; and then,
> Foaming and hurrying o'er its rugged track,
> Fell into the immeasurable void,
> Scattering its waters to the passing winds."—*Alastor.*

AILING down the Zambesi, below the entrance of the Chobe, in November 1855, Dr. Livingstone saw rising high into the air before him, at a distance of six miles, five pillars of vapour, with dark smoky summits. The river was smooth and tranquil, and the boat—in which was his stanch friend, Sekelutu, chief of the Makololo—"glided pleasantly over water clear as crystal, past lovely islands densely covered with tropical vegetation, and by high banks, with red cliffs shining through the brilliant green of the borassus and wild date palms." The traveller was not, however, altogether unprepared for the marvels that lay ahead. Two hundred miles away he had heard the fame of the gorge of Mosi-oa-Tunya—the "Sounding Smoke" —where the Zambesi mysteriously disappeared.

As the crisis was approached, the pulse of the river

seemed to quicken. It was still more than a mile in width, but it hurried over rapids and chafed round points of rock; and the most careful and skilful navigation was needed, lest the canoe should be dashed against a reef or hurried helplessly down the current. The mystery in front became more inexplicable the nearer it was approached; for the great river seemed to disappear suddenly underground, leaving its bed of hard, black basaltic rock prolonged between the well-defined banks, but with grass and trees filling the space where the water had flowed! By keeping the middle of the stream, cautiously paddling and punting from rock to rock, and taking advantage of the eddies, the canoe was grounded on a small island on the very lip of the Victoria Falls— a memorable spot, where Livingstone planted some fruit trees, and, for the only time on his travels, carved his initials, in remembrance of his visit.

Even here it could not be seen what became of the vast body of water, until the explorer had crept up to the dizzy edge of the chasm and peeped over into the dark gulf below. A river over a mile in width precipitated itself sheer down into a rent extending at right angles across its bed, and only eighty yards across! The walls of the cleft were cut as cleanly as if done by a knife, and no projecting crag broke the descent of the falling waters. Four rocks or small islands on the edge of the falls divide them into five separate cascades, and in front of each fall rises one of the tall "pillars of smoke," which are visible in flood time at a distance of ten miles. Only at low

VICTORIA FALLS.

Page 32.

water can the island on which Livingstone stood be approached; for when the river is high an attempt to reach it would infallibly result in a plunge into the thundering abyss. Against the black, glittering walls of the precipice opposite the falls, two, three, and sometimes four rainbows, each forming three-quarters of a circle, are painted on the ascending clouds of spray, which, continually rushing up from the depths below, lick off the rills of water streaming down the sides of the rock, and carry them high in air in the shape of vapour. A fine rain is constantly falling from these clouds, and the tops of the cliffs are covered with dense, dripping, evergreen vegetation. But the great sight is the cataract itself. The rent seems to be of comparatively recent formation, for the edge of the rock has been worn back only three feet. Over this the water sweeps in unbroken sheets, its glassy outer surface being only slightly indented between island and island. For eight or ten feet it falls in a crystal mass; below that it hangs like a white fleece in mid-air; and then it seems to break into detached pieces of foam that follow one another in bewilderingly swift comet-like flights, each trailing behind it a "tail" of vapour, until lost in the gloom of the chasm.

Since Livingstone's first brief visit, the falls have been more minutely examined by the doctor himself, in company with his brother Charles, and Kirk, and also by subsequent explorers, such as Mauch and Pinto,* so that we now know pretty accurately their

* The last party who visited the spot, in the close of 1879, included an Englishwoman, Mrs. Kennedy the first European lady who has seen the Victoria Falls.

dimensions and leading features. The breadth of
the river at the falls has been ascertained to be over
eighteen hundred and sixty yards, and the depth
of the precipice below the island three hundred
and sixty feet, or twice the depth of Niagara. At
the bottom of the rent, the waters that have fallen
into it both on the right and on the left rush together, and meet in the centre of the gulf, immediately beneath the island, where, confined in a space
of twenty or thirty yards, they form a fearful boiling
whirlpool. From this the stream escapes through a
narrow channel at right angles to the course of
the stream above, and turning a sharp corner,
emerges into another chasm parallel with the first,
then through another confined gap to a third chasm,
and so pursues its way in wild zigzags through forty
miles of hills till it breaks out into the more level
country of the Lower Zambesi.

The flow of the stream through this inaccessible
ravine is not so turbulent as might be imagined from
its being pent in between walls often less than forty
yards apart. It pursues its way with a churning,
grinding motion, sweeping round the sharp turns
with a swift resistless ease that indicates plainly the
profound depth of the water. It was through this
gap, caused by some unrecorded convulsion of the
earth, that the great lake that had at one time
occupied South Central Africa has been drained; and
it forms undoubtedly the most wonderful natural
feature in Africa, and perhaps also in the world.

At the Great Falls of the Zambesi we are still a

thousand miles from the sea, and many hundreds of miles from the first traces of civilization, such as it is in the Portuguese possessions of Africa. Nature has been exceedingly lavish in her gifts in the Lower Zambesi valley, giving it a fertile soil, a splendid system of river communication, and great stores of mineral and vegetable wealth—everything, indeed, suited to make the country prosperous, except a healthy climate and an industrious and peaceable population. It has been man himself that, by war and slave - hunting, has cursed it hitherto with apparently hopeless blight. Around the falls themselves are the scenes of some of the most noteworthy events in Central African warfare; and for many miles beneath them may be seen terrible traces of the devastation wrought by military ambition, which is not less the besetting sin of negro than it is of European princes.

The history of "Chaka's wars" has not yet been written, and probably never will. Nevertheless, they extended over as great an area, shook as many "thrones and dominions," as the campaigns of Bonaparte himself. Chaka was a chief, or chieflet, in Zululand, and grandfather of that Cetywayo whose ill-starred struggle with the English has cost him his country and his liberty. It is said that some shipwrecked sailors who were cast away near Chaka's kraal or village, early in the present century, entertained their host with stories of the extraordinary career of conquest of the First Napoleon, then in the zenith of his power. The black warrior was

smitten with the desire to imitate the deeds of the
man whom he resembled in some way in military
talent and boundless ambition.

By the counsel of his sailor friends he formed his
tribe into a regiment—the first of the famous "Zulu
regiments"—and immediately began to make war on
his neighbours. Their disorderly hosts could make
no stand against his disciplined array. They were
defeated, and incorporated in the Zulu army, and
Chaka went on to new conquests. To the south he
overran what is now the colony of Natal and part
of Kaffraria, mercilessly sweeping these countries of
their inhabitants, and leaving the land waste and
empty. By-and-by he held almost undisputed sway
in the coast country between the British and Portuguese possessions. His lieutenants spread the name
and fame of the Zulus far beyond these limits. One
army crossed the Limpopo river under Manikoos
and occupied the country up to the Zambesi, driving
the Portuguese under the shelter of their forts. Part
of this force, the Mazitu, or Mavitu, marched into the
unexplored region north of the Zambesi, and were
heard of as settling on a high table-land between two
great unknown lakes, which we know now to be the
Tanganyika and Nyassa; and a section of the Mazitu,
cut off from the main body on one of their plundering forays, scoured far to the north, and are now
known as the Watuta, who, under Mirambo, Stanley's
"blood-brother," are the terror of the country between Tanganyika and the Victoria Nyanza.

Still another offshoot of Chaka's power ascended

the great wall of the Drakenberg Mountains to the
temperate plateau now called the Transvaal, expelling
or slaughtering the weak Bechuana tribes that lived
there.   Finding the country too cold, and the Dutch
colonists pricking into him from the south, Mozelikatze, the leader of the Matabele, as this Zulu band was
called, moved into the country south of the Zambesi
Falls.   Ahead of Mozelikatze's army was a motley
mass of the Bamangwato and other tribes from the
skirts of the Kalihari Desert, all fleeing for bare life,
and spreading new confusion in front of them.   At the
fords of the Zambesi, below the falls, the Batokas stood
prepared to dispute the passage.   They agreed to ferry
over the fugitive Bamangwato, but landing the men
on some islands in the river, they appropriated their
women and cattle.   From another direction appeared
the war-worn and travel-stained band of the Makololo, a Basuto tribe, demanding a passage.   They had
been driven from their homes near the sources of the
Orange River; had fled, under their chief Sebituana,
across the desert; and after many adventures and
constant fighting, descended from the westward on
the Zambesi.   Sebituana was too astute and old a
warrior to fall into the Batoka trap; he kept their
chiefs and head-men as hostages until all his party
had crossed in safety.   Then drawing up his handful
of veterans on the northern shore, with the women
and children mounting guard over the cattle in the
rear, he awaited the onset of the vast host of the
Batoka nation, which was soon scattered to the winds.
Next turning to face the Matabele, who were now

close upon him, he put successfully into operation the Batoka ruse. Mozelikatze's force was destroyed piecemeal, part inveigled to an island, which they fancied was the northern bank of the stream,—the others attacked in their canoes while attempting to land. Only five, it is said, returned alive to Matabele-land. Sebituana, one of the finest characters met with in African travel, had a prosperous and peaceful close to his stormy life. The Barotse Valley and all the country up to the confluence of the Leeba had been reduced to his sway. He was idolized by his own people, and respected by the subject nations, col-lectively known as Makalaka. One of the chief objects of his ambition was gained when he saw his friend Livingstone, whom he generously entertained at his head-towns of Linyanti on the Chobe and Sechele on the Zambesi, as did his son Sekelutu after him.

The old feuds still survive. The Matabele, under Lo-Benguela, the son of their original chief, are still the ruling power on the south bank of the Zambesi. They make constant raids on the country bordering on the river, where lines of ruined villages and untilled fields are all that is left to attest where a numerous population existed. The extensive Makololo kingdom, founded on the upper streams of the Zam-besi, began to fall to pieces under Sekelutu. The tribe broke into hostile sections, and was attacked on the day of its decline by its old enemies. Its name and place have perished from among the list of African nations, and the only remnant left have escaped into the region of the Upper Shiré, where, out of gratitude mainly for the friendship of Livingstone, they act as the faithful henchmen and guardians of the Scottish missionaries who have chosen the Nyassa country for the scene of their labours.

Over the smouldering embers of these old fires the intrepid Livingstone had to pass in his descent of the Zambesi in 1856, and in his further researches in this country in company with his brother Charles and Dr. Kirk four years later. They had to tread warily and softly, otherwise the whole country might have been set in flame. To the honour of British explorers be it said, not only was no blood shed on their travels, but they succeeded in healing old-standing feuds among the native tribes whose territory they traversed.

As we descend the Zambesi, and approach the Indian Ocean, the prospect widens, and the stream gathers breadth and volume, for great tributaries flow in, especially on the right bank. The Kafue is a river hardly smaller than the Zambesi itself; some, indeed, have considered it the main stream. Its course has still to be traced, and its source, whether in some unknown lake, or in the " fountains " of which Livingstone heard, has yet to be visited. The Loangwa, met with still further down, is also a mighty river, and its banks, like those of the Kafue, are thickly populated and are rich in mineral treasure. Indeed, this part of the Zambesi valley is believed to be founded on beds of coal, which crop up here and there along the river's course—a large promise for

the future of this favoured region. The great stream
sweeps majestically on from one reach of rich tropical scenery to another; here broken up by wooded
islands, there displaying its full breadth of a mile of
shining water. Close to the shore are seen the
villages of the native fishermen, the huts and clearings for cotton and tobacco cultivation girt about on
the landward side by dense jungle of bamboo surmounted by palms, with groups of women plying their
fishing labours with wicker-baskets near the margin,
while the men venture boldly out to the mid-current
in their small skiffs. Behind the forest the green hills
slope up steeply, diversified with clumps of timber
and shrubbery, and fringed with trees on their summits. Beyond extends an undulating plain of long
grass and thorny scrub to the base of a second range
of hills—the true boundary of the Zambesi valley—
whose purple peaks may be seen from the centre of
the stream outlined against the deep blue of the
tropical sky. Now and again, on the right hand or
the left, a river valley opens up, the sides of the
gorge thickly overgrown with jungle, above which
rise the graceful, feathery tops of the palms, the vast
trunk of the baobab, or the stately stem and ash-
like foliage of the tamarind; or great meadows
extend along the margin, on which, and on the
slopes above, herds of buffaloes, zebras, water-bucks,
koodoos, and wild pigs may be seen grazing peacefully
together, with occasionally a troop of elephants or a
solitary rhinoceros. The river swarms with fish,
crocodiles, and hippopotami; indeed, Dr. Living-

stone says that nowhere on his travels has he seen such an abundance of animal life as in and around this portion of the Zambesi.

Yet it is possible even here to be, or at least to appear to be, alone. The jungle path and its high walls of grass, or the bare, wide plain with its girdle of mountains, seem the boundaries of the world. At these times, says Livingstone, a strange stillness pervades the air. "No sound is heard from bird or beast or living thing. The air is still, and earth and sky have sunk into a deep and sultry repose, and like a lonely ship on a desert sea is the long line of weary travellers." But they soon discover that they are not alone in the wilderness. "Other living forms are round us with curious eyes on our movements. As we enter a piece of woodland, an unexpected herd of pallahs, or water-bucks, suddenly appears, standing still and quiet as if forming part of the landscape; or we pass a clump of thick thorns, and see through the bushes the dim, phantom forms of buffaloes, the heads lowered, gazing at us with fierce, untamable eyes. Again a sharp turn brings us upon a native, who has spied us from afar, and creeps up with noiseless steps to get a nearer view."

Sometimes the interruption comes in an unpleasant form. Once Livingstone, walking in a reverie ahead of his party, was startled by a female rhinoceros, followed by her calf, coming thundering down along the narrow path. and had barely time to jump into the thicket to escape the charge. A few steps further

on, a thorn plucked his watch from his pocket, causing
him to look round, and there was the great beast,
standing almost at his elbow, staring spell-bound at
the new prodigy that was passing through her
domain. Occasionally a panic-stricken herd of buffaloes will make a rush through the centre of the line
of bearers and donkeys, scattering them in wild confusion into the bush, and tossing perhaps the nearest
man or animal into the air. Neither the buffalo nor
any other wild creature, however, will attack a human
being except when driven to extremity. The lion or
leopard, when watching for its prey near the spring
or above the forest track, will perhaps drop down on
a man who passes underneath; the buffalo, if it thinks
it is being surrounded, will make a mad charge to
escape; or the elephant, if wounded and brought to
bay, or in defence of its young, will turn on its
pursuer. A "rogue" elephant or buffalo, who has
been turned out of the herd by his fellows for some
fault or blemish, and becoming crusty and ill-natured
by his solitary life, has been known to make an
unprovoked attack on the first creature, man or beast,
that presents itself to his sight. Thus, one savage
old bull-buffalo furiously charged a native of Livingstone's party in the ascent of the river in 1860, and
the man had barely time to escape into a tree when
the huge head came crashing against the trunk with
a shock fit to crack both skull and tree. Backing a
little, he came on with another rush, and continued
this "butt" practice until seven shots were fired into
him. But, as a rule, every untamed creature flees in

CHARGED BY A BUFFALO.

Page 212.

terror on sighting, and still more on scenting, "red-handed man."

The voyage by river is also not without its dangers. From the parallel hill-ranges, rocky and forest-clad hills jut out at intervals, and round these the stream makes magnificent sweeps. At more than one place it is hemmed in by high walls of rock, between which it rushes in a swift current for many miles. In these gorges are to be seen the finest scenery on the river. In the time equivalent to our autumn, especially, when the deciduous trees that grow out of every cranny, and cover the rough face of the crags with a screen of foliage, are painted with gorgeous tints of vermilion and yellow, and these tints are contrasted with the dark hues of the evergreens and the fresh green of the trees that are coming into leaf, and when a setting sun is throwing its level light down the pass, the scene is such that no European imagination can picture.

But still more grand is it in the period of the rains. Every day the black clouds are seen rolling round the summits of the hills, and vomiting streams of lightning, while the thunder rumbles and echoes continually among the rocks, and rain descends in sheets, and the great river rises until its pent-up waters are tearing through the narrow gap at a height eighty feet above the ordinary river-level. The Kebrabasa Rapids, more than half-way the distance between the Victoria Falls and the sea, are the only narrows of this kind that present any serious obstacle to the ascent of the river by a steamer, and even these are believed to be passable at flood-time, when the rocky bed is "smoothed over" by the depth of water. In the ordinary state of the river the Kebrabasa Cataracts cannot be passed, although the inhuman experiment has been tried of fastening slaves to a canoe and flinging them into the river above the rapids. Near this spot Dr. Kirk had a dangerous adventure. The canoe in which he was seated was caught in the swirls of one of the many whirlpools formed by the cataracts, and drifted broadside towards the open vortex. Suddenly a great upward boiling of the water, here nearly a hundred feet deep, caught the frail craft and dashed it against a ledge of rock, which the doctor was fortunately able to grasp, and thus save himself, though he lost his scientific instruments, his notes, and his botanical specimens, the fruits of many months of travel. When Livingstone's boat, which was immediately behind, reached the spot, the yawning cavity had momentarily filled up, and he sailed safely over the very mouth of the whirlpool.

Before reaching Kebrabasa, we meet with two other noteworthy features of the Lower Zambesi—the traces of Portuguese colonization, and of the slave-trade. Nowhere, till lately, was this traffic more flourishing or more deeply rooted, or its corrupting and ruinous effects more markedly seen, than in the colony of Mozambique. Here, too, Livingstone was the champion who, almost single-handed, marched out, gave battle to the many-headed monster, and inflicted what we must hope is a fatal wound. In spite of

reiterated denials from high quarters, there cannot
be the slightest doubt that not merely Portuguese
subjects but Portuguese officials were actively con-
cerned in the operations of the slaver. They not
only winked at, but openly patronized and profited
by it. The actual slave-hunters were generally Arabs
from the coast, and Portuguese half-breeds—a race
that seems to preserve all the evil qualities of the
European and the negro. They undertook the supply
not only of the "export trade" to Madagascar, Arabia,
and Persia, which was mostly in the hands of Banians
—British-Indian subjects—but also the home market; for slavery was, perhaps still is, the basis of
society and industry throughout the Portuguese possessions in Africa.

The more extended and active the operations of
the kidnapping parties, the more hopelessly backward
became the condition of the scattered white communities. Round the forts of the Portuguese for
many days' journey were to be met with only wasted
and abandoned fields, fighting clans, and general
anarchy and decay. Their authority, it has been said,
did not extend beyond the range of their guns; and
in many places the settlements only existed on suffer-
ance of the native tribes, to whom a yearly tribute
had to be paid. For instance, the Landeens, as the
Portuguese call the Zulu tribe of the Matabele, came
down annually to Teté, on the Zambesi, clad in all
the paraphernalia of battle, to collect their black-
mail of cloth, beads, and brass wire. A refusal meant
war; and the colonists dared not increase the area of

their sugar and cotton plantations lest they should
be subjected to new exactions. Legitimate trade was
extinct, and with it true civilization.

The climate near the river is deadly. The "cach-
imba," or malarious fog from the steaming mangrove
swamps of the Zambesi delta and coast country, is
blown up the river in the mornings, bringing with
it fever and ague, that lay their enervating hands
on the mental and physical faculties of the white
men who choose this country as a residence. The
class of colonists who emigrate from Portugal to
Mozambique is not the most select. Needy adventurers, military men in disgrace, and criminals, are
types largely represented. They have neither the
inclination nor the energy to engage in the active
bodily and intellectual pursuits that alone can stave
off the evil effects of the fever, and they fall into
habits that make them an easy prey to disease.

This was not always the case in these Portuguese
possessions. At one time, before slave-trading became
the staple industry, European influence and Christian
civilization, under the pioneering of the Jesuit missionaries, extended much further into the interior
than they now do. At Zumbo, at the confluence of
the Loangwa, is still to be seen the ruined church of
one of the farthest outposts of the Jesuit fathers, its
broken bell lying half-buried in the rank weeds. At
the junction of two noble rivers, in the midst of a
beautiful and fertile expanse of green fields, undulating forest, and pleasant hills, with magnificent mountains in the background, it is a scene of utter ruin

and desolation, overgrown with thorn-bushes, nox-
ious plants, and long grass, the haunt of the hyena
and the owl,—a fit picture of the past and present
of the Portuguese colony, and of the blighting effects
of the slave-trade. The old missionaries who planted
this church were full of plans for the exploration and regeneration of Africa, and submitted
schemes with this object to their spiritual and
political superiors. Livingstone bears generous testimony — all the more rare, coming from one be-
longing to a different religious sect—to the zeal,
piety, and self-abnegation of these Jesuit priests; he
regards the calumnies circulated about them as " the
mere brandy-and-water twaddle of immoral traders."
Their plans and labours hindered the slavers' success,
and it was necessary to get rid of them by calumny
or any other weapon. With the failure of their
mission perished all true progress in discovery; and
when Livingstone visited the Portuguese colonies on
the Zambesi in 1856, he found complete ignorance of
the existence of the Victoria Falls, and only hazy
rumours regarding a lake called the Maravi, Nyanja,
or Nyassa, from which, at a distance of forty days'
journey to the northward, the Shiré, the last of the
great affluents of the Zambesi, was supposed to flow.

CHAPTER III.

"I know the secrets of a land
  Where human foot did never stray;
Fair is that land as evening skies,
And cool—though in the heart it lies
Of burning Africa."—*Peter Bell.*

THE river Shiré, which we are now about to ascend, falls into the Zambesi from the left, only some ninety miles from its mouth. Twenty years ago its course was unknown, and its banks were wildernesses untrodden by the foot of a white man. Now the stream is one of the best-known and most frequented of the highways to the Lake Regions. The Shiré is much narrower than the Zambesi, but of deeper channel, and in the upper and lower portions more easily ascended by steamers. Midway in its course, however, we meet a great impediment to the navigation of the river, and consequently to the civilization and commercial development of the regions beyond. In thirty-five miles the stream descends twelve hundred feet in a series of rapids and cataracts over a rock-encumbered bed and between sheer walls of cliff.

Beauty and use are badly adjusted on the Shiré. The scenery of the unnavigable portion of the river is full of singular and romantic beauty. In the picturesque diversity of its charms of crag and forest and rushing water it is scarcely equalled by any other part of Africa. Monotony, on the other hand, has set its stamp on the banks of the useful, slow-flowing river beneath and above. Yet the ascent of one hundred and fifty miles from the Zambesi to the cataracts is not without its attractions. The landscape is intensely and characteristically African. If the river is fringed on either shore by tall and sombre reeds, the majestic mountains that bound the Shiré valley are always in sight. A dense tropical vegetation covers these hills to the very tops, except that patches of lighter tint show where the hands of the natives have cleared the ground for the cultivation of crops of cotton, sorghum, or maize; for these healthy uplands, above the reach of the mosquito and the deadly marsh fog, and safe also, in some degree, from the ravages of the kidnapper, are inhabited by an industrious race, the Manganjas, who have made no small progress in agriculture and native iron and metal manufactures.

This whole country is favourable for the raising of cotton, which here grows a larger and finer staple, it is said, even than in Egypt. Every Manganja village has its cotton patch, where sufficient is grown for the use not only of the community but of neighbouring tribes. The demand certainly is not large, the requirements of Africans in the matter of clothing being

modest—or immodest, if you will. There is a tribe,
for instance, on the Lower Zambesi, whose name,
being interpreted, means the "Go-Nakeds." The
full costume of a "Go-Naked" is a coat—of red
ochre. Livingstone met one of their men of rank
once, and found his court suit represented by a few
beads and a pipe two feet long. Unfortunately the
Manganja, along with their ingenuity and industry
as weavers, blacksmiths, and farmers, are inordinately
fond of beer and smoking, and are great in the arts
of brewing and tobacco-manufacturing. With all
these disadvantages, however, it is pleasant to find
in one corner at least of Africa a race with both the
skill and the inclination to work, and a native industry ready to spring up into large proportions so
soon as it receives a little encouragement.

After the Zambesi has been left behind, a great
mountain called Morumbala, four thousand feet in
height, bounds for many miles the view on the
right as we ascend the Shiré. Beyond it we reach
one of the marshes or old lake-beds which form
one of the features of this valley. The bounding
lines of hills make each a semicircular curve, and
inclose a vast morass, through the centre of which
the river drains slowly between dripping walls of
sedge and mud. No human inhabitant can dwell
in these impenetrable swamps; but they are far
from empty of life. Great flights of wild geese,
ducks, waders, and other water-fowl abound here in
prodigious numbers, and rise from the brake at the
noise of the passing boat or steamer—for already

THE DENIZENS OF THE SWAMP.

steamers have ploughed the waters of the Shiré. Cormorants and fish-hawks patiently watch for their prey from the top of some tree or shrub that overhangs the water; or an antelope is seen picking its way from one oozy island to another. In the stream itself we cannot go far without disturbing the rest of some ugly saurian; or a hippopotamus, catching alarm in time, can be traced crashing its way through the reeds to a place of safety.

Consul Elton describes his passage of this "lake of mud" as a time to be remembered. The country was inundated. "Far and wide the waters stretched over the whole flat, from the margin of the hills bounding the granitic ranges north of Morumbala away to the Manganja range on the west, forming an immense expanse, here and there dotted with lines of green rushes and low trees. It was a day without a cloud—a company of distant pelicans looking like a line of breakers in the bright sunset, Morumbala purpling far away against a roseate-tinged sky, of the deepest azure overhead, the Nyanja waters of a deep amethyst colour."

But the glory of these marshes is their elephants. The Nyanja Mururu, or Great Lake, a little further on, is even a more favourite haunt for them than the Nyanja Pangolo, or Little Lake, we have just crossed with Elton. Here in 1859 Livingstone's party counted no fewer than eight hundred of these gigantic animals in sight at once; on a subsequent voyage down the river they passed "two miles of elephants." Such a spectacle as this—almost of itself worth a journey to Africa—is no longer to be seen on the Shiré. The wise animals have not been long in discovering how dangerous a new-comer the white man is in their domain, and they are too cautious now to come trooping out in herds to the bank when sounds of an unusual kind are heard on the river. The rifle has thinned their numbers, and induced many more to change their haunt; while those that remain keep in the day-time within the recesses of the swamp, where they are pretty safe from the attack of any hunter white or black. A Makololo chief who has occupied this portion of the river considers the great elephant swamp as his special preserve, and it is only by his leave—which may always be obtained by a handsome present— that the sportsman is permitted to go out after the great pachyderms. In many parts of savage Africa, indeed, the "game laws" are as strictly enforced as in civilized England, and a usual arrangement is for the hunter to share his booty with the black "lord of the soil."

Above the marshes, and just where the Murchison Cataracts begin, and river navigation consequently ends, Chibisa's village stands, or rather stood: for Chibisa and his people have given place to a new race. From this point Dr. Livingstone made three excursions in search of the "Lake Maravi," which he had heard of among the Portuguese. The first expedition threatened to end in a tragic manner. It soon became plain that the guide was leading the party quite away from the direction in which the "great lake" was understood to lie; and as they reached a lonely spot, one of the doctor's faithful Makololos came up to him, and remarked, in a matter-of-fact way, "That fellow is taking us into mischief. My spear is sharp. There is no one here. Shall I cast him into the long grass?" A gesture of assent, or even silence, and the unlucky guide would have been run through the body; but Livingstone was not the man to permit blood to be spilt, even on an apparently well-grounded suspicion of treachery. After all, it turned out to be merely a blunder, and no treachery. The party were led safely to the margin of the "great lake" of the district—the elephant marsh that they had passed some time before while ascending the river!

The second trip resulted in a discovery of an inland sea, though not the one they were in search of. Climbing over the shoulder of the high mountains east of the Shiré, the party came in sight of Lake Shirwa, lying in an isolated, pear-shaped basin, nearly two thousand feet above sea-level. Magnificent mountain scenery surrounds the lake, the waters of which, contrary to the rule in Central Africa, are salt, or rather brackish. Although the area of Shirwa is probably as large as that of all the lakes of Great Britain taken together, it is but a mill-pond compared with some of the inland seas we have visited, or with one which still lies ahead. Yet, girt in though it is with hills, it shows to one standing near its southern end a boundless sea-horizon towards the north. Opposite on the eastern shore a lofty range rises to a height of eight thousand feet above sea-level, while behind, the table-topped Mount Zomba, only one thousand feet lower, dominates the Shiré valley.

All this mountainous mass seems habitable, and, in fact, is inhabited to its very summits; and its temperate climate, healthful breezes, and freedom from malaria and mosquitoes, have led to its being chosen as the site of the Church of Scotland mission to the Nyassa country—their station, Blantyre, being named after the Scottish village where Livingstone first saw the light.

In ascending to the Nyassa, the opposite or western side of the Shiré is generally chosen, and travellers prefer to make a wide detour into the healthy Manganja uplands to struggling through the rocky, broken, and wooded country through which the river tears its impetuous way. It is delightful to breathe the bracing air of these high plains after escaping from the humid, stifling atmosphere of the valley. The change of scenery and climate puts a new life into the veins of the traveller. Many novel views of African life come under his notice among the Manganja highlands. The path up the long ascent is toilsome, but the eye is cheered by the glorious views of the deep valley lying below and the blue domes and peaks that rise ahead. The country is open and park-like, full of grand forest trees and flowing streams.

In the evening we halt at a Manganja village and receive a hearty—perhaps an uproarious—wel-

come. The villages are surrounded by thick-set
hedges of the poisonous euphorbia; and however
busy at work or at feasting the inhabitants are
inside, a guard is always kept on vigilant watch at
the entrance, to give warning if a foraging band of
Mazitu heave in sight in the mountains, or the white
robes of a party of Arab slave-hunters are seen
ascending the valley. When it is known that it is
friends who are approaching, the villagers are not
long in making amends for the shyness of their first
greetings. Mats of reeds and bamboo are spread for
the wayfarers under the shade of the banian tree at
the "boalo," an open space for the public entertainment of strangers at one end of the village, the favourite spot for lounging and smoking, and where on
moonlight nights the young people indulge in singing
and dancing and their elders in hard drinking bouts.
The whole community troop out to see the white
visitors, who are regarded with just such a mixture
of curiosity and fear as a company of Red Indians
would be looked upon by English rustics. Presents
are exchanged with the chief, and then a brisk trade
sets in, the villagers bartering food and articles of
native manufacture for beads, looking-glasses, cloth,
and other surprising products of Europe. Generally
there follow dancing, pombe-drinking, and serenading
in honour of the visitor, a homage which the latter
is often glad to escape from by strolling out for a
night-hunt for elephant or other game, or to note
down by the clear light of the moon his observations
for the day.

Soon it is time to descend into the valley, where
the Shiré is found again flowing deep and slow, as
below the falls, and opening up into a marshy lake-
let, Pamalombe, with a strong family resemblance
to the swamps of the lower river. It ought to
be recorded, in justice to African honesty, that when
the *Ilala*, the first steamer that floated on the Nyassa,
was conveyed in pieces from the Lower to the
Upper Shiré by a band of some hundreds of porters,
under Captain Young's leadership, it was found,
on putting the little craft together, that not a
single bolt or screw had been mislaid or stolen,
though the temptation to fling away or decamp
with their burdens must have sorely tried the
carriers.

Even when almost within sight of the Nyassa,
Livingstone could hear nothing of the goal of which
he was in search. The chief of the " Great Lake "
village on the Shiré told him that the river stretched
on for "two months' journey," and then emerged
from two rocks that towered perpendicularly to the
skies. " We shall go and see these wonderful rocks,"
said the doctor. "And when you see them," objected
his Makololo companions, " you will just want to see
something else." Next day they continued their
march, and before noon on the 16th of September
1859 came in sight of the lake.

Like the Tanganyika and Albert Lakes, Nyassa is
a long and comparatively narrow body of water
lying in a deep depression of the plateau of Central
Africa. From the outlet of the Shiré one can sail on

its waters for more than three hundred miles towards
the equator; but it is nowhere more than sixty miles
in width, and in some places less than half that distance across. It resembles the more northerly lakes,
the Albert Nyanza and the Tanganyika, but especially the latter, in its general shape and direction;
and it was for many years a favourite theory with
"closet geographers" that the three lakes formed
one continuous sheet of water. Such an attenuated
"river-sea," fifteen hundred miles in length and with
no breadth to speak of, would have been a new thing
in nature, and would, besides, have been an extremely
useful factor in opening up Africa. Unfortunately,
like other pretty theories, it did not stand the test of
actual examination; and we have seen that the three
lakes form parts of three different though not dis-
connected systems.

The shores of Nyassa seem to be overhung on
all sides by tall mountains, although near the southern end there is generally a margin of more level
country between the bases of the hills and the lake.
As we proceed northwards, the distinctive features
of the lake shores become more pronounced and
majestic. The strip of plain narrows until it dis-
appears. The range increases in altitude and approaches nearer, the rocky buttresses spring directly
from the water, and the torrents that rush down their
sides plunge in cascades into the lake; and the extreme northern end is encircled by dark mountains,
whose frowning tops are ten thousand feet or more
above sea-level. But when we ascend from the swel-

tering western margin of the lake to the cool and breezy heights that look down on it, we find that instead of being on the summit of a range of mountains we are only on the edge of a wide table-land. There is no steep slope corresponding to that which we have ascended so toilsomely, only a gentle incline towards the Zambesi.

On his last great expedition to Africa, Dr. Livingstone passed round the southern end of the lake, and, ascending the table-land, traced the water-shed between the lake and the streams flowing to the westward, until he descended into the valley of the Chambesi, and began that investigation of the Congo in which we have already borne him company. The contour of the country reminded him strongly of that of Southern India. There was the flat country covered with thick jungle and tiger-grass, succeeded by dense forest, gradually thinning away to clumps of evergreens as the higher levels are reached, the scattered masses of boulders, the deeply-trenched "nullahs" or water-courses, and all the other familiar features of the fine scenery of the Ghauts, while the table-land above resembled closely the high plains of the Deccan. But what a contrast in the social and industrial condition of the two countries! Instead of seeing at every step, as in India, the traces of a long-founded civilization and a race of industrious tillers of the soil dwelling in peace and security under the strong arm of the law, we meet only with anarchy, misery, and barbarism.

The whole of this region is a hunting-ground of the

Mazitu or Mavitu Zulus, whose only business is war
and pillage. The wretched inhabitants of these hills
dwell in constant apprehension of their raids. On
no night can they sleep even within the shelter of
their well-guarded stockades with the assurance that
the Mavitu will not be upon them ere morning.
Originally weak in numbers, this tribe has gathered
strength by amalgamating with themselves the clans
they have conquered. The terror which their deeds
have inspired has been heightened by their wild and
fantastic dress and gestures as they advance to battle,
and by their formidable weapons. They carry the long
Zulu shield and both the flinging and the stabbing
assegai. Their hair is plumed with feathers, and their
bodies painted in fiendish devices with red and white
clay. So abject is the fear entertained for these
redoubtable champions among the surrounding tribes,
that the mere mention of their name is enough to
make a travelling party take to their heels. Livingstone found this a constant source of annoyance and
delay. Twice it was the cause of reports of his
death being brought to this country. On the last
occasion, the Johanna men—natives of the Comoro
Isles—who formed his escort were seized with the
infectious panic, and, abandoning him in a body,
brought down to the coast the story of the explorer
having been murdered in the interior. The falsity
of their report was only ascertained after Mr. Edward
Young had made a special expedition to the Nyassa,
and learned on the spot that the intrepid missionary,
in spite of the cowardly desertion of his followers,

was safe and well, and still pushing forward towards his goal.

A disaster of a most serious nature, however, had just happened to him. Two of his bearers—slaves who had been left masterless by a Mavitu foray, and on whom the doctor had taken compassion—disappeared during the night, carrying with them his medicine-chest. "I felt," writes the traveller in his note-book, "as if I had received sentence of death." He was not mistaken. Henceforth the malarious fevers and other illnesses incident to African travel seized hold of him with a grasp which he was powerless to shake himself free from, and gradually broke down his iron constitution. To a similar misfortune may be attributed the death in the marshes of the Shiré of the good Bishop Mackenzie, who was left helpless by the upsetting of the canoe which held his drugs.

In one respect, if in no other, the Zulu "Rob Roys" of these hills have a feeling in common with the travellers and missionaries who have found their way to the Nyassa countries—they are the inveterate enemies of the slave-hunters, and will not permit these gentry to practise the arts of kidnapping and murder within reach of their spears. The eastern side of the Nyassa basin, on the other hand, is one of the principal scenes of the slave-traders' operations. In conjunction with predatory negro tribes, such as the Ajawa on the left bank of the Shiré, they have made a wilderness of all the country between the Nyassa and the Indian Ocean. Nothing can exceed

the waste and havoc they have wrought in this
beautiful and fruitful land.   The books of the
explorers are full of details of almost incredible
atrocities committed under their eyes, and which
they were powerless to prevent.   Whole populations
have been swept into the slave-gangs and hurried
down to the coast, leaving the country behind them
a desert, and their path marked by the skeletons of
those who have succumbed to exhaustion or the
cruelty of their brutal drivers.   The miserable remnant of the population roost in trees, or seek shelter
in the deepest recesses of the forests; while the jungle
overruns the fields of maize, cotton, manioc, and
sorghum, and the charred ruins of their villages.

In Livingstone's Journals we come upon such entries
as: " Passed a slave woman shot or stabbed through
the body; a group, looking on, said an Arab had done
it that morning in anger at losing the price he had
given for her, because she was unable to walk."
" Found a number of slaves with slave-sticks (logs
six feet long, with a cleft at one end in which the
head of the unfortunate is fastened) abandoned by
their master from want of food; they were too weak
to speak or say where they had come from." " It
was wearisome to see the skulls and bones scattered
about everywhere; one would fain not notice them,
but they are so striking as one trudges along the
sultry path that it cannot be avoided." This evidence
is abundantly supported by the statements of other
observers. Consul Elton describes passing a caravan
of three hundred slaves from the Nyassa, while

travelling through the clove and gum-copal forests on the Mozambique coast. "All," he says, "were in wretched condition. One gang of lads and women, chained together with iron neck-rings, was in a horrible state, their lower extremities coated with dry mud and torn with thorns, their bodies mere frameworks, and their skeleton limbs slightly stretched over with parchment-like skin. One wretched woman had been flung against a tree for slipping her rope, and came screaming to us for protection, with one eye half out, and her face and bosom streaming with blood. We washed her wounds, and that was the only piece of interference on our part with the caravan, although the temptation was strong to cast all adrift, and give them at any rate a chance of starving to death peaceably in the woods." Can it be wondered at that the pioneers of civilization and Christianity in these regions have sometimes been carried away by their feelings, and at the risk of ruining their whole plans have forcibly interfered between these Arab miscreants and their victims?

Four or five years ago, the period to which Consul Elton's accounts apply, it was computed that the Lake Nyassa region supplied some fifteen thousand slaves annually to the markets of Kilwa and other coast towns. Dr. Livingstone is convinced, from his own observations, that so far as regards the Shiré country, not a tenth of those who are captured survive the horrors of the land journey. It may be wondered how this waste of human life can go on

THE SLAVE-HUNTER AND HIS VICTIMS.

and the country not be completely depopulated. In
spite, however, of their terrible losses, there is still a
large population settled on the Nyassa. They have
been chased down from the hills by the Mavitu and the
slavers, and are huddled together on the lake margin,
where their enemies can swoop down and make them
an easy prey.

This dense population is, however, only found towards the southern end of Nyassa. Further north,
the Mavitu have taken possession of the shore as well
as the hills, and practise with equal success the voca-
tion of pirates on the water and of robbers on land.
An expedition in this direction was till lately certain
to be attended with no small excitement and danger.
If the journey were made by land, the travellers were
liable to be surprised at some point where the road
was more rocky and difficult than usual, by the
apparition of a wild-looking crew starting up from
behind boulder or tree, and advancing with bran-
dished spears and unearthly yells. White explorers
are not accustomed to turn and flee at the first alarm.
They stand, quietly awaiting the attack ; and the
Mavitu, disconcerted at conduct so utterly unlike
what they had calculated upon, run away themselves
instead. If the excursion is made by water, a crowd
of boats, pulled by swift rowers, will perhaps be seen
putting out from a secluded bight, or from behind a
wooded promontory, and giving chase to the strangers,
with loud outcries to stop. The navigators of this
inland sea, however, are missionaries and men of
peace. They have no desire to do harm to their

savage pursuers, and, secure in the speed of their little steamer and the superior range of their guns, they can afford to laugh at the attempts to capture them.

Much more serious is the danger arising from the sudden and furious storms that sweep down upon the lake from the gullies of its encircling hills. Livingstone narrowly escaped shipwreck on its waters, and from his experiences of it proposed to have Nyassa named the "Lake of Storms." An old seaman of his party, who had been over the world, and at home had spent many a squally night off the wild coasts of Connaught and Donegal, said he had never encountered such waves as were raised in a few minutes by the tornadoes on the Nyassa. Succeeding voyagers—Young, Elton, Cotterill, Drs. Laws and Stewart, of the Scottish missions—report similar experiences. Mr. Cotterill's little craft, the *Herga*, a present from the Harrow boys, was driven ashore on the western coast, June 1877, and he lost his journals, goods, and medical stores, saving only one bottle of quinine, which, remembering the fate of Livingstone and Mackenzie, he threw ashore as he neared the breakers in the darkness. The most dreaded waves on the Nyassa come rolling on in threes, "with their crests," says Livingstone, "streaming in spray behind them." A short lull follows each charge; and then another white-maned trio come rushing on and threaten to ingulf the voyagers and their frail bark.

A curious natural phenomenon has been noticed by

most observers on the Nyassa. A light blue cloud will
be observed floating for many miles over the surface
of the lake, like the trailing smoke of some distant
fire. When it is reached, we discover that it consists
of nothing else but myriads of insects, of a species
peculiar to the region, and known as the " kungo fly."
So dense is the mass that immense quantities of them
are caught by the natives and pounded into cakes,
resembling in size and shape a " Tam o' Shanter "
bonnet. They are not particular as to what they eat,
these hunger-bitten natives of the Nyassa shores.
Neither are they unreasonably extravagant in the
matter of dress, some of the tribes absolutely dispens-
ing with clothes. Their notion of making up for their
scanty attire by liberally anointing their bodies with
rancid fish oil and hippopotamus fat, and smearing
themselves with fancy designs in red and white clay,
does not recommend them to the European eye and
nostril. From our point of view, too, their attempts
at decoration by means of tattooing are in nowise
improvements, the result being to give their faces
and limbs the appearance of being thickly studded
with pimples. The most hideous device of all, however, is the " pelele," or lip ring, an ornament without which no Nyassa belle would dream of appearing
in public. This consists of a broad ring of tin or
stone, an inch or more in diameter, inserted by slow
degrees into the upper lip, causing it to stand out at
right angles to its natural direction, and revealing
beneath the rows of teeth sharpened to fine points
like those of a saw. The native ladies of rank

sometimes have a corresponding ring in the under lip, with the result that while the wearers of the single "pelele" can only lisp, the ladies of fashion are scarcely able to speak at all. Considering that these poor people have not been lavishly endowed with natural charms, the effect of their duck-like mouths may be imagined. Some handsome faces may, however, be seen among the natives of the Nyassa, and many of them, it has been observed, have regular Jewish or Assyrian features. Dr. Livingstone saw one man who bore a striking resemblance to a distinguished London actor in the part of the "Moor of Venice," while another was the exact counterpart, in black, of the late Lord Clyde.

The magnificent alpine country at the north end of the lake is, as yet, almost unknown. Consul Elton's party, while marching in 1877 from Nyassa to Zanzibar, and Mr. Thomson, on his journey from the coast to Lake Nyassa, and thence to Ujiji, in the end of 1879, are the only explorers who have crossed the chain. The sole spot where there is any level ground is a great elephant marsh. Here Elton and his companions counted no fewer than three hundred of these noble animals standing knee-deep in the swamp, the elders lazily swinging their trunks and fanning themselves with their huge ears; while the juniors of the herd disported themselves in their elephantine way, rolling luxuriously in the mud, or tearing down branches of trees in the riotous enjoyment of their enormous strength.

Elton's party enjoyed several days of most exciting

elephant-stalking in the neighbouring hills. Sallying out one morning into a part of the forest where
the great brutes were known to abound, the herd
was at length sighted; two or three of the elephants
dozing under the shade of some trees, others engaged
in munching branches, or shaking the boughs and
picking up one by one with their trunks the berries
that were scattered below. They were soon aroused
from this delightful Elysium of rest and enjoyment
by the hunters, who had crept up to within ten or
fifteen yards unseen. Singling out the biggest elephant, a huge tusker, who stood blinking contem-
platively under the shadow of a tree, Elton and his
companion, Mr. Rhodes, each planted a bullet behind
his shoulder. He trumpeted, staggered forward,
tripped over into the rocky bed of a " nullah," scrambled out on the other side, and there receiving other
two shots, crashed down lifeless into a second dry
water-course.

Chase was then given up a mountain gorge to the
next largest elephant—a cow accompanied by her
calf—which deliberately charged back at Elton, the
nearest of her pursuers. Allowing her to approach to
within about three yards, he gave her a forehead shot,
which turned her round; and then Rhodes " doubled
her over like a rabbit." The retreating herd were
pursued to the top of the pass, where the last of the
line, a big bull elephant, receiving a shot, stumbled
and fell, while Elton, with " the pace on," nearly fell
on the top of him ; " and," he says, " holding my Henry
rifle like a pistol, I shot him again at the root of the

tail. The shock was irresistible; over the edge of the ravine he went, head foremost, the blood gushing out of his trunk, and his fall into space only broken by a stout acacia, in which he hung suspended, his fore and hind legs on either side—dead." Still the hunt was continued, and on a second rocky slope a wounded elephant was found labouring up, supported and helped on by a friend on either side, while a fourth urged him on from behind with his forehead. This last faced round, and stood defiantly at bay, his ears "spread-eagled." Elton's last cartridge missed fire; Rhodes shot; a tremendous report followed; the elephant, with a groan, plunged over a cliff, and hung suspended by a thorn-tree in mid-air, like his predecessor; while Mr. Rhodes, casting his gun from him, ran down the declivity to the river, his face streaming with blood; and the survivors of the herd, toiling painfully up the mountain-side, disappeared over the sky-line, "uttering loud grumblings of disapprobation and distress." The chamber of the rifle had burst, cutting Mr. Rhodes severely in the face; and his companion endeavoured to console him by telling him that many a man at home would have given one thousand pounds for such a day's sport, and suffered the cut in the forehead into the bargain.

Such sport is, however, getting every day more difficult to obtain; for this lordly animal, the true "king of beasts," is retreating before the march of civilization, and becoming gradually more scarce even in the African solitudes. This is not to be wondered at, considering the vast numbers—probably from fifteen thousand to twenty thousand—that are killed annually for the sake of their ivory.

It may be remarked that Elton's escape from the elephant's charge was a remarkably close one. There is only one other instance known of the "forehead shot" being effectual in stopping the course of an African elephant. This adventure happened in the Abyssinian highlands to Sir Samuel Baker. That mighty hunter was at the time new to African sport, and imagining that planting a bullet in the forehead, the favourite method with hunters of the wild elephant of India and Ceylon, would be equally effectual in the case of his big-eared kinsman of Central Africa, he awaited the charge of an elephant until she was within five yards of the muzzle of his rifle. The bullet happened to strike a vulnerable spot in the skull, and dropped the animal dead; but the lookers-on for several moments regarded the hunter as a dead man.

In both these cases the elephant shot was a female, which possesses in a less marked degree than the male the solid structure of skull that, along with their immense ears, convex foreheads, and greater size, distinguish the African from the Asiatic variety. When not struck in a vital spot, the elephant is remarkably tenacious of life; and Livingstone tells how he fired twelve bullets into one that had fallen into a hole, and had about a hundred native spears sticking in him, and next morning found that the animal had scrambled out and escaped into the forest. Perhaps the most perilous experience that

ever befell a white hunter when after elephants
occurred to Mr. Oswell, far to the southward, on the
banks of the Zouga.   Chasing an elephant through a
thorny thicket on horseback, he suddenly found the
animal had wheeled round and was bearing straight
down upon him.   Attempting to turn his horse, he
was thrown, face downwards, before the elephant.
Twisting round, he saw the huge fore foot about to
descend on his legs, parted them, and drew in his
breath, expecting the other foot to be planted on his
body; but saw the whole of the " under-side " of the
huge creature pass over him, and rose unhurt to his
feet, saved almost by miracle.

But this has carried us far away from the elephant
marsh, from the borders of which Messrs. Elton,
Cotterill, Rhodes, and Hoste made their ascent of
the mountain barrier of Nyassa.   The lowest pass
over the Konde, or Livingstone range, is eight thousand eight hundred feet above sea-level; and the ascent
embraces every variety of climate and scenery, from
stifling tropical swamp to breezy moorlands of fern
and bracken, carpeted with wild thyme, daisies, dande-
lions, and buttercups, like our English hills at home.
From the top a magnificent landscape is viewed.
Elton says : " The country we have passed through is
without exception the finest tract in Africa I have
yet seen.   Towards the east we were walled in with
mountains rising to a height of from twelve to fourteen thousand feet, inclosing undulating, well-watered
valleys, lovely woodland slopes, hedged-in fields, and
knolls dotted with native hamlets.   There is nothing

to equal it either in fertility or in grazing land in Natal, the reputed 'garden of South Africa.' It is the most exceptionally favourable country for European semi-tropical cultivation I have ever seen." Against European cultivation there stands the fact that the land is already taken up in every direction by the natives.

A more serious obstacle still to the development of this beautiful highland region is probably the exceptionally deadly climate of the country through which it must be approached. Already many precious lives have been sacrificed in the attempt to open up the Nyassa. Livingstone, we saw, got here his "death-sentence." The German Roscher, who, travelling in the guise of an Arab from the east coast, viewed the lake only two months later than the great missionary, was basely murdered at a little village near its shores. Bishop Mackenzie is buried in the Shiré swamps; and near him lie nearly the whole staff of the University Mission to this region, all stricken down with marsh fever. Thornton, the intrepid companion of Livingstone on his first visit to the Nyassa, after having ascended half-way up the snow-capped mountain Kilimandjaro, far to the northward, returned to this quarter, only to die at the foot of the Murchison Rapids. Mrs. Livingstone, the devoted wife of the missionary, rests under a gigantic baobab tree a little way below the Shiré mouth; and near her grave is that of Kirkpatrick, of the Zambesi Survey Expedition of 1826. Another baobab, in Ugogo, shades the resting-place of Consul Elton, whom we saw, full of life and hope, at the head of the pass overhanging the north end of the lake. Only a few marches to the northward of the pass, while toiling across a droughty plain, and weak from hunger and fever, he succumbed to sunstroke, and a most useful and promising career closed at the early age of thirty-seven. Still younger was Mr. Keith Johnston, the news of whose death, from dysentery, while leading an expedition from Zanzibar territory to Nyassa, reached this country only in September 1879. Dr. Black is buried on Cape Maclear, the rocky promontory cleaving the southern end of the lake, where the Free Church of Scotland Mission Station of Livingstonia has been planted; and the little cemetery already contains at least other two English graves.

The Scottish mission stations on the Shiré and Lake Nyassa are not the only outposts which Christianity has planted in the far interior of the "dark continent." Similar colonies, for the moral improvement and industrial training of the natives of Africa, have been placed on the shores of the Victoria Nyanza and Tanganyika by the London and University Missionary Societies. The example is being followed by similar associations in France and America; and the Zambesi country has been mapped out for a renewal of the long-abandoned work of the Jesuit fathers. Science, commerce, and philanthropy have enlisted by the side of religion in the task of opening up Africa. The chief outlets of the slave-trade have at length, it is hoped, been closed, thanks mainly to the efforts of England, and the hearty co-operation of the governments of Portugal, Egypt, and Zanzibar.

Even the lighter graces and charms of civilized life are beginning to manifest themselves; for we find the sultan of Zanzibar entertaining his guests to dinner served in European style, in company with ladies, and to the music of an orchestra playing choice selections from Beethoven and Weber. News has been received that a Scottish lady, Miss Waterston, has safely ascended the Shiré to Livingstonia, to take her share in the good work along with her fellow-countrymen. Schemes have been proposed, and in some cases even surveys made, for the flooding of the northern deserts; for the irrigation of parts of the Kalihari; for the draining of the pestilential coast lands; for the development of cotton, sugar, and tobacco cultivation on the Zambesi; for the opening up of the Congo region as a market for the produce of the Manchester looms; for the building of a line of railway from Egypt to the Nile lakes, and of another from the east coast to Tanganyika; for the running of steamers on the great inland rivers and lakes; and for laying a telegraph wire from end to end of the continent. Many of these plans are doomed to disappointment, but not all; and with one at least—the construction, under English surveyors, of a regular road, available for wheeled conveyances, from Dar-es-Salaam on the coast of Zanzibar to the interior—some practical progress has already been made. Roads are the great need of Africa, and their formation would effectually kill the slave traffic.

A score of expeditions are attacking the still unvisited parts of the continent from different directions, and soon there will be little new country to
explore.   The English, the French, the Portuguese,
the Germans, the Belgians, the Italians, and the
Egyptians are all enlisted in the task.   Two English
travellers have started from the Cape with the
courageous intention of surveying the unvisited
country from the Zambesi to the Albert Nyanza.
Mr. Thomson has carried out successfully the task of
opening up a way from Nyassa to the coast, which
cost the life of the lamented Keith Johnston; and
from Nyassa has made his way to Tanganyika,
which he reached only two days earlier than a party
from Livingstonia led by Mr. James Stewart.   The
King of the Belgians' mission is making good progress more to the northward; and the Indian elephants accompanying it have passed scathless
through the dreaded clouds of the tsetse fly.   Expe-
rienced elephant-tamers will follow them, and an
attempt will be made to enlist the wild African
elephant in the service of man.   In the Galla country
south of Abyssinia, Marquis Antonori's Italian expedition is pursuing its researches; Rohlfs, Schweinfurth,
and other German explorers, are continuing, or about
to resume, their labours on the eastern side of the
Sahara: and in an opposite quarter two French explorers have just revealed the sources of the Niger in
the Kong Mountains, east of Gambia.   The French are
also busy on the Ogowai, and the Portuguese in the
country inland from Angola.   And, perhaps most

important of all, Mr. Stanley, with a fully equipped party, has recently entered the Congo River, disappearing in its dark jaws, from which he had so much trouble in escaping in 1877. In a word, the mystery and gloom that have so long shrouded the interior of Africa are dissipating like clouds before the rising sun, and a brighter era for that dark, unhappy land seems about to begin.

THE END.